einstein's
refrigerator

AND OTHER STORIES
FROM THE FLIP SIDE
OF HISTORY

by steve silverman

**Andrews McMeel
Publishing**

Kansas City

01 02 03 04 RDH 10 9 8 7 6 5 4 3 2

Library of Congress Cataloging-in-Publication Data
Silverman, Steve, 1963–
Einstein's refrigerator : and other stories from the flip side of history /
by Steve Silverman.
    p. cm.
Includes bibliographical references.
ISBN 0-7407-1419-8 (pbk.)
    1. Curiosities and wonders. 1. Title.

AG243 .S56 2001
031.02–dc21

                                                    2001022201

Book design by Holly Camerlinck

contents

part 5: incredible stories of survival . . . 125

part 6: unbelievable! . . . 143

introduction

Welcome to my book! I am well aware that most people want to breeze right through the Introduction, so I will keep this short.

What you are about to read is the very best of my Useless Information Home Page. I started the Web site just prior to the explosion of the Internet while people were still holding to the steadfast rule that the Net was not a place for commercial exploitation. Intended solely as an exercise to learn the newly invented HTML coding, I never thought that anyone would ever see my work. Without any idea of what to place on a Web page, I turned to a few of the crazy stories that I had e-mailed to a friend. Just a bit of cutting and pasting, coupled with some basic Web page coding, and the site was born. The title Useless Information was thrown on for lack of a better idea.

As I had expected, no one initially looked at the Web site. My total number of visitors during the first two years was just over thirteen thousand. I then went to visit my parents over one July Fourth holiday and came back three days later to find that my readership had doubled. I found out through one of my e-mail messages that Yahoo had chosen my Web site as their pick of the week. That just started the ball rolling. Millions of readers and many awards later, traffic to the Web site continues to grow exponentially each year.

I assure you that every story contained in this book is absolutely true. Mankind is a very unusual beast and has created a history that is full of the wonderful and the truly bizarre. My research into each of the topics has been very time consuming due to the obscure nature of every story. Many times the most often told version of a story is not always the correct one. When sources have been contradictory or sketchy, I have chosen what I felt was the best inference that could be made. Readers have also been very kind about pointing out minor errors and sources of additional information.

My process of selecting story topics is nearly always the same. When I come across a tidbit that fascinates me, I then present it to my students. Having taught high school science students for so many years, I can testify to the fact that they are the toughest of all audiences to please. Some of the stories prove to be duds and are quickly dropped. Those that fascinate my students are added to a long list of possible subjects. As information is gathered, a file folder is started. The final stage is the hardest part: the actual writing of the stories.

Thanks must go to all of the people whom you have probably never heard about: my family, friends, students, and readers for their constant support and words of wisdom. In particular, I need to personally thank my best friends Barbara Roosevelt and Jamie Keenan for all of their helpful suggestions and editing of my writing.

I doubt that any one of these stories will make any difference in your life. These are certainly not the inspirational type of stories that Oprah would ever choose to do a show on. Yet, if in the end you have a smile on your face, then I will know that I accomplished my goal. So, sit back, get some milk and cookies, and relax. Enjoy this journey through the other side of history.

PART 1:

you've got
to be kidding!

mike, the headless chicken

he really was a chicken running around with his head cut off

The e-mail message seemed innocent enough. A reader simply asked "Ever heard of the story posted here at this link?" and offered a hyperlink to another Web page. I clicked and came across a story that I was sure had to be pure fiction. The only problem is that the story appears to be totally true.

This is the story about Mike the Chicken. Mike, of course, was not your ordinary chicken. No, not ordinary at all. You see, Mike was a headless chicken. If you want to be really specific, Mike was actually a headless wyandotte rooster.

I should point out that Mike wasn't always a headless bird. In fact, he was born 100 percent normal, complete with a head in Fruita, Colorado.

On September 10, 1945, Mike's short five-and-a-half-month life was about to take a turn for the worse. On this day, Mike received a death sentence. His owners, Lloyd and Clara Olsen, decided that it was time to slaughter a group of birds, sell some, and prepare others for themselves. Out to the hen house they went.

Watch out, Mike!

As you can probably imagine, Mr. Olsen was the one whacking the heads off while Clara plucked and cleaned the birds.

Bash! Down came the ax and off went Mike's head.

Mike's head was surely dead. Mike's body was not.

Now I know what you are thinking—it is well known that chickens will run around frantically when their heads are chopped off. That's probably where that old expression comes from. And, everyone knows that a headless chicken just can't survive more than a few moments.

Apparently, Mike forgot to read the rulebook for playing the game of Life. His head may have been lying on the floor, but he had no problem standing up and strutting around as if nothing had actually happened. The next day, Mike was still flopping around, so Lloyd decided to feed him to see how long he could keep the bird alive. Through his open esophagus, Mike was fed a mixture of ground-up grain and water with your typical eyedropper. Little bits of gravel were dropped down his throat to help his gizzard grind up the food. Day after day he continued to gain weight.

Mike the Headless Chicken with his supposed head. (Waters collection photograph, http://miketheheadlesschickenbook.com)

Mike could easily balance himself on the highest perches without falling. His crowing consisted of a gurgling sound made in his throat. Mike even attempted to preen his feathers with his nonexistent head. It seems that Mike could do just about anything that any other chicken could do, if you excluded all of the functions of his head. Apparently he never noticed that he was missing a major body part.

As I'm sure you can imagine, headless chickens are not an everyday event. In the tradition of that famous huckster Barnum, there was money to be made in this oddity. A promoter by the name of Hope Wade came along and convinced Lloyd that Mike would be a big draw in the sideshow circuit. Miracle Mike, as he soon came to be known, toured up and down the West Coast of the United States. The head was stored in a canning jar and traveled along with Mike. (Actually, a cat ate Mike's head. Some other poor chicken's head was pickled in the jar.) Just six weeks after his beheading, Mike was featured in a *Life* magazine article and his fame grew. Anyone could pay to get a look at Mike for just 25 cents. At the height of his popularity, Mike was raking in a cool $4,500 per month, which was no small potatoes in those days.

And if there was money to be made, there were also copycats. Other people in Mike's hometown began to chop the heads off their own chickens in an attempt to get in on the scheme. One copycat headless rooster was named Lucky and he managed to live for eleven days before bashing himself into a stovepipe and dying. (Lucky wasn't that lucky after all.) Several other headless chickens lived for a couple of days.

So how was Mike able to survive? Scientists examined him and determined that Mr. Olsen had not done a very good job of chopping Mike's head off. Most of the head was actually removed, but one ear remained intact. The slice actually missed the jugular vein and a clot prevented him from bleeding to death. Apparently, most of a chicken's reflex actions are located in the brain stem, which was largely untouched. Mike was also examined by the officers of several humane societies and was declared to have been free from suffering.

One serious problem that Mike commonly experienced was that he would start to choke on his own mucus. The Olsens came up with the simple solution of using a syringe to suck the mucus out. But, one day tragedy struck. Mike was traveling back home to Fruita and was roosting with the Olsens in their Phoenix motel room. They heard Mike choking in the middle of the night and quickly realized that they had left the syringe at the sideshow the day before. Miracle Mike was no more.

The exact date of Mike's belated departure from this world was never recorded. Years later, it was estimated, based on

Lloyd's information, that Miracle Mike died in March 1947. Eighteen months living without a head could be considered a world's record. Yet, Lloyd didn't want to admit that he had accidentally killed the bird, so he claimed that he had sold the bird off. This little white lie is the reason that many of the stories printed about Mike claimed that he was still touring the country as late as 1949.

But wait, the story is not over! Mike actually has his own holiday! On May 17, 1999, Mike's hometown of Fruita held the first "Mike the Headless Chicken Day" in honor of one of its most famous citizens. Some of the events included the 5K Run Like a Headless Chicken race, egg tosses, Pin the Head on the Chicken, the Chicken Cluck-Off, and the classic Chicken Dance. The food offerings included—you guessed it—chicken, chicken salad, and the like. Let's not forget the great game of Chicken Bingo in which the numbers were chosen by where chicken droppings fell on a numbered grid.

If you are interested, Mike the Headless Chicken Day is an annual event. As peculiar as it is to describe, it actually sounds like a great time. And it's all done in celebration of the life of one lucky bird named Miracle Mike.

Useless? Useful? I'll leave that for you to decide.

fartman

you can really earn a living releasing foul-smelling gas!

Unemployed? Looking for a career change? Do I have a job for you!

You can earn big bucks releasing farts. (Move over Howard Stern.)

However, you better be good at it. People won't pay to see any old amateur farter. They want a professional. A guy like Joseph Pujol, better known to his audiences as "Le Pétomane."

Now, I must point out that I was never really sure if this story was actually true. Then, I was having dinner with a gentleman from France several years ago. Before I could even finish asking him about the story, he cut me off and confirmed that Pujol is, in fact, a very famous man in France.

On with our story.

Little Joey was born on June 1, 1857, in Marseilles, France, and it didn't take long for him to discover his hidden talent. As a young boy, he went with his parents to the seashore. While swimming, he decided to hold his breath and dive down deep.

This dive would make history. Suddenly, Pujol felt a rush of icy cold water enter his bowels and rush up inside his intestines. (Sounds like fun!) Little Joey was so frightened that he ran out of the water to his mom. All of a sudden, he felt the water rush out of him and spill all over the beach. (Ooh, the embarrassment.)

Pujol eventually grew up and was called into military service. While there, he got into one of those typical all-male gross-each-other-out-type conversations. He mentioned his boyhood experience, and of course, they asked for a demonstration.

On their next furlough, Pujol took a trip to the sea and tried it again.

It worked!

Pujol eventually started to perfect this skill. Using a basin of water, he practiced this great art in private. He controlled the rate of intake and outflow by flexing his anal and abdominal muscles. He could shoot a stream of water to a distance of four or five yards.

Soon he was able to advance to the next stage—using air instead of water. The art of the fart had begun!

After leaving the Army, Pujol went to work in the family bakery. In the evenings he moonlighted at local music halls by singing, playing trombone, and doing comedy routines. In private, he entertained his friends using his other wind instrument, so to speak. They suggested that he add it to his act.

He perfected his act and rented a space in Marseilles in which to perform. They did heavy promotion, making the show a sellout every night.

Pujol began his act by walking out dressed elegantly in silks and starched white linen. Once the opening monologue was complete he leaned forward, hands on his knees (of course with his butt facing the audience), and started a whole series of imitations. He managed to keep a straight face the whole time. The audience couldn't. They laughed so hard that many women in tight corsets passed out. The theater was forced to hire nurses for each show.

He would imitate a little girl by emitting a delicate little fart. He would release a long slide to imitate his mother-in-law. Let's not forget cannon fire, machine guns, and thunder. He even could play musical scores. His act lasted an hour and a half.

Quite the talented guy! I'm quite envious of his fine skill.

For his finale, he invited the audience to fart along at the appropriate times. It was one big fart-a-thon. (It must have smelled great.)

Of course there were skeptics. Pujol was forced to submit to medical examinations to prove that he was for real.

Pujol was France's highest-paid entertainer at the time, but he eventually retired from the profession and returned to the world of baked goods. He raised his family and died in 1945 at the age of eighty-eight. The medical faculty at the Sorbonne offered 25,000 francs for the right to examine his body when he died, but his family refused the offer.

And so ends the life of the world's greatest farter. It was a gas.

Useless? Useful? I'll leave that for you to decide.

the collyer brothers

but where was langley?

Move over Frasier and Niles Crane. You've got company. There actually were two brothers who were more eccentric than you could ever hope to be.

The two brothers that I'm talking about were born into the very best of circumstances. They were descendants of one of New York City's oldest families. Their ancestors came to America aboard the *Speedwell* way back in the *Mayflower* days. Their father, Dr. Herman L. Collyer, was a wealthy and well-known Manhattan gynecologist. Susie, their mom, was an educated woman who had a great interest in the classics. In 1881, the couple was blessed with the birth of their first son Homer, who eventually went on to get a degree in engineering. Next came Langley, who was born in 1885 and as an adult received a degree from Columbia University and became an admiralty lawyer.

Then, in 1909, the boys' bubbles burst. As unlikely as it sounds for that time period, the couple decided to separate. Dad moved out and the two siblings, both in their twenties, chose to continue living with Mom. Life wasn't too bad for them. At the time, they were living in a luxurious three-story mansion at Fifth Avenue and 128th Street.

But times change. Their mom died. The Harlem neighborhood started to decay. Poverty was the norm. Crime was rampant. The Collyer brothers, as a result, retreated deeper and deeper into seclusion from the rest of the world.

But, let's face it. Lack of interaction with the rest of the world can make people very strange. It's the kind of weirdness that brings people like Homer and Langley fame.

Over time, the brothers boarded up their windows. They placed booby traps all over their home to ward off intruders. They even had the gas, water, and electricity turned off in their mansion. For a while, Langley tried to produce his own energy using an automobile engine. Water was fetched from a park four blocks away. They cooked and heated their big home with a small kerosene heater. When Homer went blind in 1933, Langley formulated a "cure" that consisted of a steady diet of one hundred oranges per week, black bread, and peanut butter. (Sounds as if it would work to me.)

Very strange.

In 1942, the Collyer brothers made the newspapers. They had defaulted on the mortgage on their home and the bank came knocking on the door. The Bowery Savings Bank began eviction procedures and a work crew was sent over to clean up the yard. Langley Collyer started screaming at the workers and the police had to be called in. The cops ended up smashing down the front door, only to encounter a wall of junk piled up to keep people out. Silently, Langley wrote out a check for $6,700 and paid off the mortgage in full.

He ordered everyone off his premises and that was the last that the world heard of the Collyer brothers.

That was until Friday, March 21, 1947, when a man named Charles Smith called police headquarters at 10 A.M. claiming "There's a dead man in the premises at 2078 Fifth Avenue." To this day, the true identity of "Charles Smith" remains a mystery.

A patrolman was dispatched to the scene, but he couldn't get into the building. There was no doorbell or phone. The doors to the mansion were locked. The basement windows were broken, but protected by iron grillwork. An emergency squad of seven men had to be called in.

So, what would you do in this situation? There's supposedly a dead body in this house and you can't get in. The most obvious thing to do would be to break the door down, which is exactly what they did. The entranceway, however, was blocked by a wall of old newspapers, folding beds, one half of a sewing machine, folding chairs, boxes, part of a wine press, and many other pieces of junk.

It was clear that the police were not getting through the front door easily.

The policemen decided upon another approach. They got a ladder and threw it against the building. They attempted to go through a second-floor window instead.

Well, they were out of luck. The brothers had piled even more packages and bundles of old newspapers behind the window opening. The police started to pull all the junk out and throw it down to the street below. Out came countless old newspapers, empty cardboard boxes that were tied with rope, the frame of a baby carriage, a rake, two umbrellas tied together, and other stuff.

Once some of the material was cleared away from the window, a patrolman was able to step inside. Using a portable light, he shoved aside more bundles of rubbish and found Homer Collyer sitting on the floor with his head between his knees. The tiny old man's matted gray hair reached to his shoulders. He was clad only in an old, ragged blue-and-white bathrobe.

Dr. Arthur C. Allen, the assistant medical examiner, confirmed that it was the body of Homer Langley and that he had been dead about ten hours. His proclamation was "As Coroner, I must aver, I thoroughly examined him, and he's not only merely dead, he is really most sincerely dead." (Well, maybe those were not his exact words.)

As the crowd outside the mansion swelled to over six hundred people, everyone started to wonder where Langley was. Could he be wandering around the city on errands? Could he still be in the house in hiding? Was he the one who called in the tip to the police? No one was really sure.

The following Monday the police began their search of the house for the missing brother. Out came more junk—gas chandeliers, the folding top of a horse-drawn carriage, a rusted bicycle, three dressmaking dummies, a sawhorse, a doll carriage, a rusted bedspring, a kerosene stove, a checkerboard, a child's chair, countless old newspapers, pinup girl photos, and so on.

But where was Langley?

The next day the police returned and pulled out an intricate potato peeler, a beaded lampshade, the chassis of an old car, children's toys, and over six tons of newspapers, magazines, and wood.

But where was Langley?

On the third day even more stuff was taken out of the house. Anything deemed worthless was just tossed out the window to the ground below. Items of value were placed in storage.

But where was Langley?

On the fourth day the police continued the removal of junk from the home. In the search for Langley, they found an assortment of guns and ammunition. Near the location of Homer's death, an assortment of bankbooks was discovered for a total worth of just $3,007.

But where was Langley?

On Saturday, March 30, a report came in that Langley had been seen boarding a bus for Atlantic City. The hunt for the missing brother temporarily shifted to the New Jersey coast, but there was no sign of him.

So, where was Langley?

Monday came around and, again, the police removed more junk from the home. This included over three thousand books, plenty of outdated phone books, a horse's jawbone, a Steinway piano, a primitive x-ray machine, and more bundles of newspapers. By the end of the day a total of over nineteen tons of junk had been removed from the first floor of the house alone!

So, where the heck was Langley?

And the search continued. Every day more stuff was taken from the home. Old medical equipment, human medical specimens, a wide variety of musical instruments, and (of course) more bundles of old newspapers.

Enough of this garbage. Where was Langley?

On April 3, 1947, the police thought that they had found him. A body was found floating in Pugsley's Creek in the South Bronx. The body sure looked like the missing brother, but it was later identified as a man named Thomas Lynch, who had disappeared earlier in the week.

Come on already, where was Langley?

Day after day, more and more junk was removed from the home. By Monday, April 7, 103 tons of essentially worthless garbage had been taken from the house. (Does the typical house even weigh that much?)

By now you know what the next line is going to be. And you must be sick of my asking it.

Where was Langley?

Luckily, that is the last time that I have to say it, because on Tuesday, April 8, 1947, the body of Langley Collyer was finally located. Believe it or not, he was less than ten feet from where his brother Homer had died. His body was partly decomposed and was being gnawed on by a big ugly rat. A suitcase, three metal bread boxes, and—you guessed it—bundles of newspapers were covering his body.

In the end, investigators concluded that Langley was asphyxiated after one of his booby traps collapsed on him. They believe that he was crawling through the tunnel-like maze in an effort to bring food to his paralyzed and blind brother Homer.

With no one to feed him, Homer essentially starved to death.

The brothers' estate was valued at $91,000 in real estate and $20,000 in personal property. What was salvageable from the 136 tons of junk that had been collected sold for less than $2,000 at auction. Their once beautiful mansion was condemned, torn down, and is now a parking lot.

Now we have just one unanswered question. What was the deal with all of those newspapers? Langley provided an answer in a 1942 *New York Herald Tribune* interview. "I am saving newspapers for Homer, so that when he regains his sight he can catch up on the news."

Sadly, he never had the chance to catch up on the news. Instead, they both became the news.

Useless? Useful? I'll leave that for you to decide.

michael malloy

possibly history's most bizarre murder scheme

You probably have never heard of Michael Malloy. After all, he never did amount to much in life. He was a sixty-year-old unemployed fireman in the Bronx, New York. Malloy emigrated to the United States from Ireland, but that really has little to do with this story. All you really need to know about this guy was that he was an alcoholic—a man who would do anything for a drink.

In fact, it was Malloy's drinking problem that got him into trouble. He became the victim of one of the most unusual murders in American history.

So let's set our watches and clocks back to January 1933 and make a visit to a speakeasy operated by a guy named Anthony "Tony" Marino. Should you ever be in the neighborhood, be sure to make a visit to its former location—3804 Third Avenue. By anyone's standards, this place was a dump. Dingy, dirty, and raw would be the best way to describe the establishment.

A speakeasy war was taking place at this time and Marino was in need of some quick cash. Along with a customer named Francis "Frank" Pasqua, an undertaker who spent most of his time embalming himself with alcohol, he came up with the perfect quick-cash solution. They decided to take a life insurance policy out on someone and then bump the poor guy off.

Perched at a broken-down poker table in the rear of the

speakeasy, the two men peered out into the main room. Their eyes quickly focused on a guy named Michael Malloy. Malloy was the perfect choice because he was a drunk with few known relatives or close friends. No one would ever miss him.

The plan was set into action. Three policies were taken out on Malloy under the pseudonym Nicholas Mallory. The first was for $800 from Metropolitan Life. Two additional policies of $494 each were taken from Prudential Life. The policies had a double indemnity clause; if Malloy just happened to have an accidental death, then double the value would be paid.

Now all they had to do was bump Malloy off. They assumed that this would be an easy task. A few too many drinks and he would be a goner.

They figured wrong.

Their first move was to relax all credit restrictions against Malloy. He could drink all that he wanted. So, for the first week he drank like a fish from the time he wandered in until he staggered off at night. Each day the "Murder Trust," as they would soon be known in the tabloids, would wait for news of Malloy's death.

Instead, Malloy would wander back into the bar each day to get more drinks.

The members of the Murder Trust knew they had a problem. They had invested a lot of money in the insurance policies and the alcohol, yet Malloy seemed no closer to death.

So they decided to spike Malloy's drinks.

The speakeasy's bartender, Joseph "Red" Murphy, just happened to be an unemployed chemist. He was skilled at adding small amounts of chloral hydrate to drinks to knock out unwanted customers. For a $100 cut in the action, Murphy agreed to help bring an end to Malloy's existence. The only problem was that Murphy was out of chloral hydrate. Instead, he substituted antifreeze from his 1927 Model-T Ford as the poison of choice. Night after night he added the antifreeze (poisonous wood alcohol at that time), but this had no effect on Malloy. Day after day he was back, refreshed and wanting more to drink.

The group then tried adding turpentine, horse liniment, and even rat poison at various times to Malloy's drinks. Any of these ingredients would do the ordinary man in, but Malloy was a hardened alcoholic and he could somehow tolerate these poisons.

Through his alcoholic daze, Pasqua recalled that he had heard about a man who had died from consuming either raw oysters or clams that had been soaked in whisky (it seems to me that many people do this each day with no problem). They decided to go one better—they saturated an equal amount of oysters and clams in the deadly antifreeze broth. Malloy downed piles of this delectable meal. To their surprise, Malloy was back the next day hungry for more.

The Murder Trust then came up with what they felt was a surefire killer. They opened a can of sardines and allowed it to spoil for about one week. Once it took on a really bad stench, they prepared a delectable sardine sandwich. Of course, no sandwich is complete without minerals, so Marino ground up the tin can and added the fine shavings to the sardines. As an added measure, they threw in some chopped-up pins to this concoction.

I'm sure you can guess what happened next. Malloy downed the sandwich, licked his fingers, and left. Did he die? Of course not. He wandered in the following day looking for more.

Most people would have given up at this point, but not the members of the Murder Trust.

Enter the fourth member of the Trust. Hershey "Harry" Green was a Bronx taxicab driver and a frequent customer of the speakeasy. Once again, Malloy was filled with alcohol until he passed out. At this point, they loaded Malloy into Green's taxicab and took him to a deserted area of Claremont Park. They carried Malloy's limp body out of the cab and laid him down behind a row of shrubbery. They opened up his shirt to the raw elements and poured water all over his exposed flesh. A good bath never hurt any drunk, but it just happened to be fourteen degrees below zero Fahrenheit that night. They were positive that Malloy would freeze to death.

Not the indestructible Michael Malloy. He somehow survived and wandered into the bar the next day complaining of a slight chill.

They decided it was time to get an expert. For another $100 cut, they hired a hitman named Anthony "Tough Tony" Bastone to do the job.

Tough Tony decided that they should just murder Malloy out-and-out. He had a plan that would make it look like an accident, meaning double the insurance money.

The scheme was to run Malloy down with Green's taxi. Just like clockwork, they got Malloy drunk and threw him into the taxi, drove to a deserted intersection, and carried him out of the vehicle. Green then accelerated his taxi up to forty-five miles per hour and raced down the street. As the cab approached, Malloy somehow managed to stumble to safety at the last moment. (This guy really did have the luck of the Irish!)

Once again, they placed Malloy back in the vehicle and drove to a more remote area. This time they carried out their plan and Malloy was crushed to death by the force of the car.

At least the Murder Trust thought that he was dead. They saw his body crushed. There was no way that they could have messed up this time. Or could they have?

The Murder Trust members checked the obituaries daily searching for Malloy's pseudonym. They then scanned the papers for stories about a hit-and-run in the Bronx. No luck.

Well, if he wasn't dead, then Malloy had to be in a hospital. They knew that they had hurt him badly. Red Murphy was then sent on the mission of checking all of the hospitals and morgues for his dear "missing brother." Once again, no luck.

Clearly, Malloy was dead. Yet, without a death certificate or obituary notice, the Trust could not claim the insurance money.

So they decided to bump off another guy named Joseph Patrick Murray. Murray certainly fit their bill—he was someone they felt nobody would miss. The Trust got Murray drunk and tried the old run-him-over-in-the-taxicab routine. They ran Murray over and were about to turn around and do it again for good measure, but they were frightened away by the lights of a passing motorist.

The real trick was how they were going to pass Murray off as the fictitious Nicholas Mallory. Pasqua placed letters addressed to Mallory in Murray's pocket. In addition, there was a card indicating that Pasqua be called in case of an accident—in which case he would identify the body as being of one Malloy—I mean Mallory.

As you can imagine, this plan also backfired. Murray somehow survived and spent fifty-five days recovering in Lincoln Hospital.

To make matters even worse, about three weeks after the initial "accident," Michael Malloy came wandering into the speakeasy. He had somehow survived.

His "friends" showed great concern for his health. (Yeah, right.) When they questioned where he had been, Malloy said that an automobile had hit him. (Do you think they were shocked by his answer?) He had suffered a concussion of the brain, fractured skull, and a fractured shoulder. He had spent the time at Fordham Hospital, but due to some sort of clerical error, the hospital had failed to register him as a patient.

The Murder Trust was really thrown into turmoil. Tough Tony made it clear what had to be done. They had to kill Malloy ASAP. No more trying to be clever; they had to bump him off and get the insurance money.

Bastone challenged Malloy to a drinking bout. As usual, poor Malloy was given more of the dreaded wood alcohol and eventually fell into a state of unconsciousness.

Daniel Kreisberg, the sixth and final member of the Trust,

was now brought in on the scheme for fifty bucks. (A measly amount for taking someone's life.) Kreisberg and Murphy carried Malloy up to a rented room at 1210 Fulton Avenue. Red Murphy then proceeded to hook a rubber hose up to a wall gas jet and place the other end in Malloy's mouth. But, the hose did not reach and they had to pull Malloy off the bed and drag him closer to the hose. Kreisberg turned the gas on, claiming during the trial that he "could hear the sizzling sound" of the escaping vapors. They had finally succeeded in doing what they had set out to do so many weeks before. They killed Malloy on February 22, 1933.

Getting rid of Malloy's body was simple. If you remember from earlier in the story, Pasqua was an undertaker. He took care of everything from this point on. An ex-alderman named Dr. Frank Manzella was called in to write a phony death certificate declaring that Malloy had died from lumbar pneumonia with alcohol as a contributing factor. Pasqua placed Malloy in a cheap ten-dollar coffin and buried him in a charity grave in the Ferncliffe Cemetery in Westchester County. Of course, he wrote out a bill for $400 worth of services.

Clearly, this is not the end of the story. It seems that these guys started to argue over how the loot was to be split. Taxicab driver Green demanded additional reimbursement for the damage to his cab and sought out the opinion of complete strangers. Tough Tony and Kreisberg openly talked to others about their part in the murder. As with all stories that involve criminals with loose lips, the tale eventually found its way to the police. After two weeks of investigation the arrests were made.

During the process of probing into this scheme, the police learned of the death of a hairdresser named Mabelle Carlson nearly a year before. Carlson died on March 17, 1932. The coroner ruled that it was death due to terminal bronchopneumonia complicated by acute and chronic alcoholism. It was later learned that Marino had gotten Carlson drunk until she passed out. He took her up to his room and laid her down on the bed and stripped her naked. Marino then poured water all over her body and opened the windows on a cold night. Unlike the resilient Malloy, she froze to death. Marino just happened to be the beneficiary of her $800 life insurance policy. (Does this story sound shockingly similar to another one that you recently learned about?!?)

The details of this story came out at the trial of the killers. In addition to all that has been described above, two other interesting details were brought to light. First, it seems that Malloy had suffered an incredible blow to the head. If he had survived the gas poisoning, he would have been blind in his left eye. Second, it

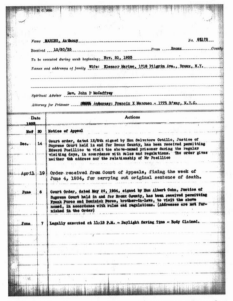

The actual prison record from Sing Sing prison for Tony Marino, showing that he was legally executed for the murder of Michael Malloy on June 7, 1934, at 11:13 P.M. (New York State Archives)

was revealed that the Murder Trust had arranged for Malloy to be shot with a machine gun, but, in typical Malloy fashion, he somehow eluded the trap that the gang had set up.

In the end the sentences were handed down. Harry Green, the taxi driver, turned state's evidence and went to jail on a lesser charge. Dr. Frank Manzella served prison time for being an accessory after the fact. Frank Pasqua, Anthony Marino, and Daniel Kreisberg got zapped in the electric chair at Sing Sing prison on June 7, 1934. Joseph Murphy (Murphy, Marino, Malloy, Mallory, Murray—there are a lot of M's in this story) also went to the chair on July 5, 1934.

So what happened to Tough Tony Bastone? Apparently, there was a bit of a squabble over the division of the insurance money and he was shot dead about a month after Michael Malloy's death in the same speakeasy. Of course, all of the defendants claimed at trial that Bastone was the one who coerced them into killing Malloy. (It's very easy to blame the guy who can't be there to defend himself.)

And the insurance money? The Trust collected the $800 from Metropolitan Life Insurance Company. However, they held off putting in the claims for the two Prudential policies. It seems that the main beneficiary, Murphy, was in jail as a material witness to Tough Tony's murder, and his partners in crime did not want to bring attention to their scheme.

Sounds like the script for a good Hollywood comedy. On the other hand, nobody would ever believe it . . .

Useless? Useful? I'll leave that for you to decide.

the rooster booster

the feathers will be flying!

Imagine sitting down one day and reading an absurd story on the Internet about how the Federal Aviation Administration (FAA) requires all new airplane engine designs to undergo an oddball test where chickens are shot from a cannon toward the engines.

You do a bit of searching, but authenticating such a crazy story seems impossible. It's apparent that this story has been floating around the Net for quite some time. You give up in frustration and decide that this tale must not be true.

Then, you are flipping through the TV channels the next night and, amazingly, there they are shooting chickens at an airplane engine in a totally unrelated story. Actual video to prove that such a thing is done.

Well, life is full of such strange coincidences. This actually happened to me. Just what are the chances that I could come across this obscure topic two days in a row?

Now that I've given you the background about how I got to this point, I am sure that you are wondering about the Rooster Booster.

So here goes . . .

Have you ever been driving down the road in your car and witnessed a head-on collision between your windshield and some unfortunate bird?

Splat!

But cars go at a relatively slow speed when compared to that of an aircraft. Imagine hitting a bird while going at Mach 1 (that's the speed of sound). You'll experience more than just splat. Chances are, if your plane is poorly designed, that severe damage could occur.

This is no minor situation we are talking about here. The U.S. Air Force estimates that there are between 2,500 and 3,000 bird strikes to their planes alone each year. This produces a large amount of damage, estimated to cost the service between $50 and $80 million annually. Occasionally, these incidents can also result in human death. (I will spare you from viewing some of the bloody photographs several readers have sent me on this story!)

Clearly, something needed to be done to reduce this damage.

Although the exact origins of the Rooster Booster are difficult to trace, it appears that the device first became popular during the Vietnam War in the early 1970s. The military's F-111 aircraft was equipped with terrain-following radar, which allowed the plane to cruise at only several hundred feet in the air. I think that you can see the problem here. If you're zipping along at a low altitude, you are going to smash into a large number of birds and cause a lot of damage.

As a result of this damage during the Vietnam conflict, as well as normal nonmilitary flights worldwide, aircraft builders started to test their designs for resistance to bird strikes.

Well, what better way is there to test for bird impact damage than to shoot a real bird at high speed at real aircraft?

In reality, they could shoot any bird at the test designs. They could use ducks or turkeys (and they do). One would guess that swans and pink flamingos could also be used, but this would anger many people. Let's face it, when it comes to choosing a bird, the lowly chicken becomes the prime candidate. Chickens are cheap and common, so they are ideal for the bird test.

Now before you start screaming about cruelty to animals, I

should point out that the testers use dead birds. You know, carcasses. The birds were on their way to someone's dinner table, but instead they took a detour to become a projectile in the Rooster Booster.

Yes, these are heroic chickens. They didn't just become someone's meal—they helped to save a life (unfortunately it was not their own).

Apparently, the majority of these chicken cannons work off compressed air. Unfortunately, birds don't make tight seals with the wall of the cannon, so the bird is placed in a container called a sabot, a French term meaning "shoe." When the gun is fired, the sabot (which is typically made from balsa wood, foam, or fiberglass) is mechanically stripped away by blades and the bird becomes a dangerous projectile.

Duck! Incoming!

There are strict guidelines when it comes to using the Rooster Booster. First, the bird must weigh either four pounds (military testing) or eight pounds (FAA testing). Second, the bird must be thawed (fresh or thawed, not frozen as some strange stories floating the Net seem to report). Third, the bird must be unplucked—it must be as realistic as possible.

The chickens are loaded into their sabot and fired from the gun (actually anything big enough to shoot a chicken should be called a cannon) at a very high velocity. Different guns are capable of shooting at different speeds, but they all seem to be around 125 to 180 miles per hour. There are reports of higher speeds of 500 miles per hour or more, but it's hard to ascertain whether they are realistic numbers or not.

The chickens are shot at various components of the aircraft. Generally, these targets tend to be windshields, fragile wing components, and engines.

The testing of the engines is one that needs to be seen to believe. All new engine designs must pass this "chicken ingestion test" (and other tests) in order to receive FAA approval.

When the chick hits the fan, so to speak, it disintegrates almost immediately. Shredded feathers and body parts seem to fly in all directions. Certainly sounds disgusting, but it's better than the turbine blade doing the same and bringing an end to many human lives.

So the next time that you are flying in a plane while on your way to some nice tropical paradise, be sure to give thanks for that chicken that gave up his or her life for the sake of human safety.

Useless? Useful? I'll leave that for you to decide.

ballooning

up, up, and away in my beautiful lawn chair

Did you ever have one of those nights where you have one hundred channels and there is still nothing on? It was on one of these nights that I stumbled across a show called *Junkyard Wars: Flying Machines*. The hosts had a team of washing machine repairmen take on a team of psychologists to see who could create a better flying machine. The rules were fairly simple. Each team had ten hours to construct a flying machine out of anything in the junkyard. The team that could keep a man in the air the longest was the winner.

So, this got me thinking. Let's suppose that I could build an aircraft in ten hours. Would I really want to risk my life by getting into such a thing? I think not. Then I started thinking about a man named Larry Walters, who built his own flying machine years ago and took a most unusual ride in the sky.

Larry, unlike the junkyard teams, had spent an entire lifetime planning his flight. It all started when Larry was eight or nine years old and his parents took him to Disneyland. Larry was captivated by a large bundle of Mickey Mouse balloons that a Disney employee was carrying. At that moment, Larry knew that he wanted to someday attach himself to balloons and fly high up into the sky.

During his teen years, Larry experimented with small balloons by filling them with hydrogen gas. (If you recall, the *Hindenburg* exploded because it was filled with hydrogen. This was not a safe thing for a teenager to do.) Later, as Larry was completing his stint as an Army cook in Vietnam his actual plan fell into place.

On July 2, 1982, Larry decided, after many years of waiting, to put his plan into action. He started to assemble his craft, fittingly titled *Inspiration,* in the backyard of the home of his girlfriend's mother in the suburban Long Beach area of California. Using fifty-five cylinders of helium, Larry inflated forty-two seven-foot-diameter balloons that he had obtained from a local Army-Navy surplus store. Just imagine the sight of these balloons floating at nearly 150 feet above the ground! It must have been an amazing sight to see.

Because Larry had spent so many years preparing for his flight, he was well equipped for just about any emergency. He had a compass, an altimeter, a two-way radio, a flashlight, a first aid kit, and a pocketknife. Larry was very creative and attached eight plastic jugs filled with water to the sides of his craft for ballast. In another stroke of genius, he took along a BB gun, which he intended to use to shoot out the balloons so that he could slowly glide back to the ground.

Perhaps the most unusual thing about Larry's flying machine was the design of its basket. Actually, it was the craft's lack of a basket that captured one's attention. Instead, Larry opted for a lawn chair that he had purchased from Sears for $109.

Larry put on his parachute and climbed into the *Inspiration.* The craft was tethered to a friend's car, which was designed to limit Larry's height to about fifty feet. This would allow Larry to get a feel for the craft before he actually cut loose. Larry's ascent, however, was much faster than he had ever expected and the rope snapped.

Larry was headed for the sky!

His original flight plan had been to max out at eight or nine thousand feet and then travel approximately three hundred miles to the Mohave Desert and land. Having risen much more quickly than he had anticipated, Larry scrapped these plans and decided that he just wanted to enjoy the ride. Just imagine the view from those heights without the walls of any aircraft to block your vision! It must have been incredible.

Larry's major concern was not about landing, but to avoid going too high where the air was thin and the temperature low. At about fifteen thousand feet, Larry decided that it was time to descend a bit. As planned, he fired his BB gun at the balloons and punctured seven of them. Just at the moment that he was gazing down to check his altimeter, a gust of wind hit the chair and the gun fell out of his lap. He watched helplessly as the gun got smaller and smaller as it fell to the ground. (Imagine the lawsuit if someone had actually been standing under the gun when it hit!) While Larry had prepared his craft for nearly every conceivable thing that could go wrong, he somehow overlooked the possibility of losing the gun overboard. A simple piece of string attached to the gun would have been all that was needed.

Yet, even with the loss of the gun, Larry was not worried. His craft climbed a bit higher, topping out at 16,500 feet. Do a little bit of math and you will quickly realize that Larry and his lawn chair were floating at an altitude of over three miles! At one point, Larry flew into the airspace of the Los Angeles airport and was spotted by both Delta and TWA pilots.

The *Inspiration* then began to slowly descend to the ground. For some reason, the *Inspiration* started to pick up speed during the last two thousand feet. Larry cut off all of his ballast in an effort to slow the craft down. He ended up bouncing off the roof of a home and tangling the craft's tethers in some power lines. This placed Larry and his chair at about eight feet above ground. Power to the community was shut off for about twenty minutes while he was cut down. (He was lucky that he wasn't zapped.) Larry then gave his chair away to some kid in the street and autographed pieces of his balloons.

Larry may have completed his flight successfully and safely, but the Federal Aviation Administration was not pleased. On December 17, they fined Larry $4,000 for violating four aviation regulations, which included flying a vehicle that was not certified as air worthy. Larry had invested his entire savings in the flight and was unable to pay. After a bit of negotiation, the FAA reduced the fine to $1,500 for operating an unsafe vehicle. (I guess any future Wright Brothers can forget about trying out experimental aircraft designs.)

Larry became an instant celebrity as news of his flight spread around the globe. He appeared on *The Tonight Show* and *Late Night with David Letterman*. Yet, Larry was never able to profit from his flight. With the onslaught of the Internet, Larry's story has been widely circulated. He was awarded the Web's 1997 Darwin Award for "stupidity above and beyond the call of duty."

Sadly, Larry committed suicide in October 1993. No suicide note was found, but his death most likely had little to do with his flight years before.

One more unfortunate piece to this story: Larry theoretically holds the altitude record for clustered balloon flight, but this goes unrecognized since his flight was unlicensed and unsanctioned.

Useless? Useful? I'll leave that for you to decide.

PART 2:

oops!

the great boston molasses tragedy

history's stickiest disaster

This is a story that I had heard when I was very young, but I cannot place its origins. It was one of those stories that I always assumed was pure fiction until I stumbled upon it once again more than twenty years later.

Clearly (since you can read the title above), I am talking about the Great Molasses Flood that swept through part of Boston, Massachusetts, on January 15, 1919.

At this time in history, molasses was America's primary sweetener. It was used to make all types of cookies, cakes, breads, and especially rums. Due to its popularity at the time, there were many molasses factories, warehouses, and storage tanks lining the shores of Boston. After all, Boston was considered to be the distilling capital of the United States.

To tell this story, we are concerned only with one of these facilities—a large storage tank located in Boston's north end—near the sites where the world-famous Faneuil Hall, Quincy Market, and the New England Aquarium stand today.

This was no small tank of molasses. The cast-iron tank had an eighty-foot-diameter base and stood over fifty feet tall. Estimates of its capacity range from 2.2 to 2.5 million gallons!

And we all know where this story is going.

A sudden thunderous cracking sound was heard. The tank exploded and all the molasses began to flow down the city streets.

The actual wall of molasses was estimated to be from fifteen to thirty feet high and moved at twenty-five to thirty-five miles per hour in the area around the tank. The depth was only (only?!!) several feet in the surrounding area. You could not outrun this thing. (This brings to my mind images of people running down the street trying to outrun Godzilla.)

There was no chance of saving anyone in its destructive path. Anyone who attempted to go near the sticky goo got stuck in it himself and became part of this sticky tsunami. I bet that it could have sucked the boots right off your feet.

The flood killed 21 people and injured an additional 150. Some were suffocated, some cooked, and others were swept by the wave into the harbor. I guess you could say that these unfortunate people were molassassed to death. Not exactly how I wish to go.

The wave also destroyed millions of dollars' worth of property. Homes and warehouses were swept off their foundations. Even part of the city's elevated train line was destroyed when a portion of the molasses tank knocked out a few of the supporting girders.

Once the flood stopped, cleanup began. They could not remove the trapped horses from the sticky mess, so they had to shoot them. Freshwater from the fire hydrants would not wash away the molasses, so salt water from the harbor had to be sprayed on the land.

It took over six months to remove the molasses from the cobblestone streets, theaters, businesses, automobiles, and homes. The Boston Harbor was also stained brown for six months (must have made for a beautiful photo opportunity).

Believe it or not, there were reports that the molasses actually continued to creep out of the ground and cracks in the sidewalks for thirty years! Others claim that you can still smell traces of it on a very hot day in the city.

So what happened to cause this mess?

No one is really sure, but there are two theories:

First, it was believed that the tank was overfilled because of the impending threat of Prohibition. The tank was poorly engineered and cracked open because of the extra pressure exerted by the extra goop.

An alternative explanation has to do with the weather that day. On the prior day, the temperature was only two degrees Fahrenheit above zero. On the day of the accident, it had quickly shot up to an unseasonably warm forty degrees. Some believe that this caused rapid expansion of the molasses and overstressed the tank.

Whatever the cause, this mess tied up the court system for years. Over one hundred lawsuits were filed against the tank's owners, the United States Industrial Alcohol Company. The company claimed that it was not responsible because the explosion of the tank was clearly the work of a saboteur. With no proof to support the company's claim, the courts ruled in 1925 that the collapse was due solely to structural weakness. The distillery had to pay out nearly $1 million in fines.

This accident is certainly one that will stick in the minds of Bostonians for many years to come.

Useless? Useful? I'll leave that for you to decide.

citicorp tower

watch out for the leaning tower of citibank

If you have been to New York City at some point in the past twenty years, you almost certainly know all about the Citicorp Tower. The building can't be missed. As it is the only skyscraper with a triangular roof, it seems to have been made in honor of Mr. Pythagoras (of right-triangle fame) himself.

What few people seem to know, however, is that this gigantic structure came very close to falling down on the people of Manhattan Island. If it hadn't been for the keen observations of a New Jersey college student, tens of thousands of lives might have been lost in one single catastrophe.

So, let's start with a little background on this superstructure.

I guess that we could go all the way back to Otis' invention of the safety elevator, but we'll save that story for another time. Instead, let's go back to 1977. The mighty city of New York was on the verge of bankruptcy and crime was riding high. No one saw much future in this place. (Some still don't.)

One bright spot in 1977 was the opening of the Citicorp Tower. This fifty-nine-story behemoth was an engineering marvel that seemed to offer a glimmer of hope to a quickly fading city. Built for a mere $175 million, the building was extremely light for its size and included many engineering innovations.

Although the skyscraper's roofline is its most prominent feature when viewed from the distance, it is really the base of the building that is most interesting. It seems that the tower's designers were faced with a unique challenge—St. Peter's Lutheran Church was located at one corner of the building site. The church agreed to allow Citibank the right to build in the air above the church, but not the ground that the church stood on. In exchange for these "air rights," Citibank agreed to build a new church on that corner to replace the old dilapidated building.

What to do? What to do?

Leave it to the engineers to come up with the perfect solution. They simply cut off the corner support of the building, so that the building would hover some seventy-two feet out over the church. In fact, while they were at it, they decided to remove all four corner supports on the building. By performing some mathematical trickery, the supports were moved from the four corners in toward the center of each side of the building. Yes, the building today stands on just four narrow nine-story-high stilts, one located in the center of each wall of the skyscraper. (Spooky, huh?)

Okay. So now let's zoom a little bit closer to the present. It's June 1978 and the Citicorp Tower has been standing for about a year. The grand opening celebration is over and all those involved in the project have moved on to bigger and better things.

The phone rings in the office of William LeMessurier, the project's chief structural engineer.

Rinnggg!

The call was from that college student in New Jersey briefly mentioned at the top of this story. It seems that the student's professor had given him a project. It was one of those dreaded research paper–writing assignments that kids love so much. He was to study the Citicorp Tower and reduce his findings to words.

The student told LeMessurier that his professor claimed that the support columns were put in the wrong place. They should have been placed at the corners of the building, not the center (no, duh!).

Of course, LeMessurier explained to the student the rationale behind placing the supports in the center of each building face, and assured the student that all was safe. In fact, LeMessurier explained that the positioning of the supports made the building ideal for withstanding quartering winds—winds that come in at a forty-five-degree angle and hit two sides of the building simultaneously.

LeMessurier hung up the phone. LeMessurier was sure that the building was well designed and was not about to fall down. He decided to use the topic of conversation in a structural engineering class that he taught. Since New York City building codes required only calculations on perpendicular winds, none were ever done for quartering winds. So, LeMessurier sat down to figure them out.

Of greatest interest to LeMessurier was one of the building's unique design features. Anyone who has done even the simplest construction knows that the strongest way to reinforce a rectangle is to place a diagonal brace across it. LeMessurier did just that on a grand scale. To strengthen the structure's shell, a series of diagonal steel girders (which, when grouped together, formed a series of chevrons) were incorporated.

LeMessurier's calculations showed that half of the building's chevrons would encounter a 40 percent increase in stress when hit by a quartering wind.

This increase in stress could easily be absorbed into the building's original design. But there was a problem. LeMessurier had learned just several weeks earlier while working on plans for a new tower in Pittsburgh that his design for the Citicorp Tower had been slightly modified. It seems that LeMessurier had specified welded joints for the diagonal braces, but the contractor chose weaker bolted joints instead. The bolting was significantly cheaper and helped to speed up completion of the building. From an engineering standpoint, this was a legitimate substitution, and there was no need to consult LeMessurier.

Unfortunately, LeMessurier's calculations did not confirm this. It seems that the use of bolted joints translated a simple 40 percent increase in stress into a 160 percent increase.

Uh-oh!

Could the bolts handle this kind of force?

LeMessurier found out the answer on July 26, 1978. Wind tunnel tests were conducted at the University of Western Ontario with a scale model of the tower. With the reduced strength of the Citicorp structure calculated in, it was determined by LeMessurier that the building had a 50 percent chance of blowing down if exposed to a sustained wind speed of seventy miles per hour for five minutes. This is the type of wind that statistically occurs every sixteen years—in what we common folk call a hurricane.

Let's hear a really big UH-OH! We could have a disaster on our hands.

LeMessurier had some tough decisions to make. He could keep quiet and hope that nothing ever went wrong with the building. On the other hand, coming forward and stating the problem straight out could have great consequences for LeMessurier—almost certain bankruptcy due to litigation and loss of his professional reputation.

Luckily for New York, LeMessurier chose the correct path. He decided to blow the whistle on himself.

LeMessurier met with lawyers from his insurer, and they called in additional engineers to assess the problem. It was determined that Citibank officials had to be notified, but getting in touch with top officials at a big corporation is simpler said than done. One could just go to a Citibank teller window and blurt out, "The building is going to collapse and kill thousands of New Yorkers!" but that probably would start a citywide panic. Instead, LeMessurier had to make his way through the many layers of administrative staff to get to the head honchos.

Eventually, building architect Hugh Stubbins was able to get an appointment with Citicorp's executive vice president John S. Reed. Reed had an engineering background and was involved in the skyscraper's design and construction. Reed immediately realized the urgency of the situation and arranged an appointment with Citibank's chairman Walter Wriston.

LeMessurier told the Citicorp brass that he had a plan to fix the building, but time was of the essence. It was August 2 and the hurricane season was fast approaching. There was no assurance that the building could actually survive.

LeMessurier proposed that H-shaped steel "bandages" be welded on to each of the building's two hundred dangerous joints. This would allow the building to withstand winds that only occur every thousand years or so.

But LeMessurier also had one more thing on his side. Since the building was so light, it had a tendency to sway a great deal in the wind. He designed a device known as a tuned mass damper to moderate the tower's sway. The damper was the first of its kind and relied on Newton's First Law—the principle of inertia. The damper consisted of a four-hundred-ton concrete block that slid on a steel pan filled with oil. Clearly, they could not depend on the damper to save the building, but it could help it withstand stronger winds. Backup generators were installed for the damper to ensure that it would not fail during a blackout.

Citibank knew that the problem had to be kept a secret to avoid panic. Yet, they needed to come up with a way to evacuate midtown Manhattan in a moment's notice.

Three organizations were contacted: the Red Cross, the National Weather Service, and the Mayor's Office of Emergency Management.

The Red Cross calculated that a catastrophic collapse could result in a domino effect that would affect up to 156 midtown blocks. Officials secretly proceeded to map out all of the activities of the people around the Citicorp Tower. To collect these demographics, the Red Cross volunteers were told that they were doing a marketing survey. In those days, before high-speed computers, the Red Cross volunteers had to catalog the city street by street and block by block using only clipboards. They had no idea what they were really collecting the data for.

On Tuesday, August 8, Citibank posted notices stating that the wind bracing system was going to be reinforced and that the engineers on the project had assured them that there was no danger.

Construction began.

As soon as the office staff left each night, the crews ripped the fireproofing gypsum off the wall so the welders could install the two-inch-thick plates. By 4 A.M. the welders stopped and the cleanup crews came in. By the time the office staff came back in the next day, one could hardly tell that any work had been done—everything was practically back to normal.

But one strange effect could be seen across the city skyline. One could easily see the glow of the welders diagonally up and down the chevrons. This strange sparkling glow was initially reported by the *Wall Street Journal* on August 9, but no follow-up was done. Everything was still a secret.

That was until the *New York Times* called LeMessurier's office inquiring into what was going on. LeMessurier realized that the cat was about to be let out of the bag. However, he lucked out. When LeMessurier went to return the phone call at six o'clock, he heard a message that said that the *New York Times* had gone on strike just at that moment. The secret remained.

Weather predictions were filed four times a day from the National Weather Service at the RCA Building.

On September 1, it was predicted that Hurricane Ella was moving up the East Coast and was headed for New York. Could this be the storm that blew over the building? Should they evacuate the city? Luckily, before a final decision was made, the hurricane moved out to sea and the alarm was called off.

Work continued until mid-October, without a storm with high-magnitude winds ever occurring. In fact, in all the years since, no storm of high magnitude has touched Manhattan.

Clearly, the building survived (check it out for yourself if you don't believe me), and the evacuation plan that was actually known as Plan No. 828 was never used.

To think that it took a phone call from a college student to save the lives of thousands of people. . . .

Useless? Useful? I'll leave that for you to decide.

the lake peigneur
disaster

and away goes the lake down the drain!

Flashback to Thursday, November 21, 1980. This day may seem of little importance to you. If you were living near New Iberia, Louisiana, however, you will probably never be able to forget the strange series of events that took place on this date.

Initially, this day started out just like any other day. (All strange stories seem to begin this way.) The sun was just about to rise on Lake Peigneur. Located on this 1,300-acre lake, which was just three feet in depth, was Jefferson Island, home to the beautiful Live Oak Gardens botanical park. Contrasting with this natural beauty were the many oil and gas wells dotting the lake's perimeter.

Here we find the Wilson Brothers Corporation, which had been hired by Texaco, drilling a test hole at Well Number 20. The first 1,227 feet of drilling seemed to go very smoothly. But something started to go haywire at 1,228 feet.

The five-man night crew had run into some drilling problems during their shift and decided to stay awhile until the seven-man day crew showed up at 6 A.M. By 6:30 A.M., the drilling rig started to tilt slightly. The crew suspected that the drilling rig was collapsing under their feet. They radioed

Texaco's district office in New Iberia about the problem. Both crews decided to abandon the platform and head for shore, which was just two hundred to three hundred yards away.

The water of Lake Peigneur slowly started to turn, eventually forming a giant whirlpool. A large crater developed in the bottom of the lake. It was as if someone pulled the stopper out of the bottom of a giant bathtub.

The crater grew larger and larger, eventually reaching sixty yards in diameter. The water went down the hole faster and faster. The lake, which was connected by the Delcambre Canal to the Gulf of Mexico some twelve miles away, caused the canal to lower by 3.5 feet and to start flowing in reverse. A fifty-foot waterfall (the highest ever to exist in the state) formed where the canal water emptied into the crater.

The whirlpool easily sucked up the $5 million Texaco drilling platform, a second drilling rig that was nearby, a tugboat, eleven barges from the canal, a barge loading dock, seventy acres of Jefferson Island and its botanical gardens, parts of greenhouses, a house trailer, trucks, tractors, a parking lot, tons of mud, trees, and who knows what else. A natural gas fire broke out where the Texaco well was being drilled. Let's not forget the estimated 1.5 billion gallons of water that seemed to magically drain down the hole. (Does the Coriolis effect come into play here?) Of course, there was the great threat of environmental and economic catastrophe.

I'm sure that by now you are wondering what could cause this mess? And, since the Earth is not hollow, where did all that water go?

It was actually quite simple: Texaco was drilling on the edge of a salt dome. Unfortunately, salt domes tend to be the home of salt mines. Yes, they drilled right into the third level of the Diamond Crystal Salt Mine that had been operating nearby.

It's not that Texaco was unaware of the salt mine. They knew it was in the vicinity, but they did not know that it was exactly where they were drilling. Texaco had contacted the U.S. Army Corps of Engineers, which had, in turn, contacted Diamond Crystal. Unfortunately, the necessary communications failed to take place and the disaster occurred.

Of course, freshwater in a salt mine is a big problem. When the water comes in contact with the salt, the salt dissolves. And, of course, in a salt mine, most of the sodium chloride (salt) is removed and pillars of salt are left in place to support the roof above. (Most of the tunnels in this mine were as wide as four-lane highways with eighty-foot-high ceilings.) Dissolve these pillars and all the land on the surface will start to cave in. Which, in turn, means that the small hole that Texaco drilled became bigger and bigger as the salt dissolved.

I should mention that there were fifty workers in the mine when the disaster occurred. An electrician working in the mine noticed that water was starting to collect at his feet and heard the gurgling of water over his head. He quickly called in the alarm. Luckily, the mineworkers had just held a safety drill on the previous Saturday, so they knew exactly what to do. The lights were flashed on and off three times and a paging system was used to contact all workers about the evacuation order.

Nine of the miners were working in the 1,300-foot third level. They immediately hopped into the mine's steel cage and were hoisted to safety.

The remaining forty-one workers were working at 1,500 feet below the surface on the fourth level. They quickly ran up to the third level, only to find that the corridor to the elevators was blocked by waist-deep water. The workers were able to use some of the carts and diesel-powered vehicles in the mine to drive to the 1,000-foot level, where they caught an elevator to the surface.

That was one close call! Of course, they all now had to face an even tougher challenge—they were suddenly unemployed. After two days of water pouring in, the mine was totally filled and the heavy-duty equipment used to mine the salt was destroyed.

Although three dogs perished, there was no loss of human life. One man, Leonce Viator Jr., was actually out fishing with his nephew Timmy on his fourteen-foot aluminum boat when the disaster struck. The water drained so quickly that the boat got stuck in the mud and they were able to walk away! Luck was certainly on their side. (Did you ever notice how people get more upset when a dog dies in these oddball stories? They seem unmoved when it's a person.)

Federal mine safety experts from the Mine Safety and Health Administration found it impossible to determine who was to blame for the salt dome collapse, mainly because all of the evidence went down the drain. Of course, a disaster like this leads to endless lawsuits. Diamond Crystal sued Texaco. Texaco countersued Diamond Crystal. The Live Oak Gardens sued both Diamond Crystal and Texaco. One woman sued Texaco and Wilson Brothers for $1.45 million for injuries (bruised ribs and an injured back) received while escaping from the salt mine. In the end, Texaco and Wilson Brothers agreed to pay $32 million to Diamond Crystal and $12.8 million to the Live Oak Gardens in out-of-court settlements.

Eventually, the land above the salt mine stabilized and life returned to normal. The Live Oak Gardens was rebuilt on its remaining land. The environmental catastrophe that was anticipated at the time of the accident never materialized. Nine of the barges eventually popped back up like corks, but the drilling rigs and tug were never to be seen again. The salt mine was permanently closed, but most of the workers were able to find suitable employment. The torrent of water helped dredge Delcambre Canal and made it two to four feet deeper. And of course, the three-foot-deep Lake Peigneur was now thirteen hundred feet deep!

The moral of this story? The next time you need a well drilled, make sure someone has checked to see what you are drilling into!

Useless? Useful? I'll leave that for you to decide.

the rainman

don't wish for too much of a good thing

Maybe it is just my imagination, but there seems to be a drought every summer. No matter how much it rains every fall, winter, and spring, those guys on the news are always declaring a water emergency within a couple of weeks of the onset of summer.

As taxpayers, we should demand that our politicians do something about this recurring problem. Just spend the money and fix it.

You're probably sitting there right now scratching your head. You're wondering how in the world could those guys in Washington ever solve the water problem. Well, I am here to tell you that not only is a solution theoretically possible but it has actually been done.

Take the case of a man named Charles Mallory Hatfield. Charlie, who has long since passed on, was technically known as a pluviculturist.

A pluvio Who? What?

That's just science speak for a rainmaker, although Hatfield preferred the term moisture accelerator. Hatfield is perhaps the most famous of all of the rainmen who ever walked this blue planet that we call home.

He was born in Fort Scott, Kansas, in 1875. His family eventually settled on a farm in Southern California in the 1880s. He quit school after the ninth grade to become a salesman for the New Home Sewing Machine Company. Around this time, Hatfield began his first experiments in rainmaking. By 1902, he had perfected his rainmaking techniques which involved a secret mixture of some twenty-three chemicals (some have reasoned that it was hydrogen and powdered zinc) and large galvanized evaporating tanks.

In February 1904, he promised to deliver to the citizens of Los Angeles a whopping eighteen inches of rainfall between that December and the following April. Perched up on a twenty-foot-tall wooden tower, Hatfield released plumes of his secret recipe into the air above La Crescenta. Almost immediately, it started to rain. The Weather Bureau claimed that Hatfield's rain was really part of a much larger storm, but that didn't stop Hatfield from taking claim. This success allowed Hatfield to achieve folk hero status in the region and to pick up the nickname the "Rainmaker."

He was rehired in December to bring more rain to the drought-stricken region. Hatfield guaranteed the people of Los Angeles that he could deliver at least eighteen inches of rain by late April. By the middle of March he was only a fraction of an inch short of his goal. For his efforts, Hatfield received $1,000 in cash plus even more priceless publicity. Hatfield took to the lecture circuit and took on the misnomer of professor.

In 1905, Alaska was suffering from a major summer drought and the miners were complaining. Oddly, they were not upset because they were thirsty or because their crops wouldn't grow. No, it turns out that they needed the water to collect gold. Since most of the gold in Alaska was in the form of placer deposits, the miners needed high running waters to separate the gold particles from the rest of the junk rock.

There was obviously something wrong in this neighborhood. So who were they going to call?

Ghostbusters, of course.

Oops . . . Wrong story.

Of course, the miners contacted America's premier moisture accelerator—Charles Hatfield.

The deal that Hatfield made with the Alaskans was actually quite simple. A board of seven men would decide how much rainfall Hatfield would have to provide. If he met their goal, then he would receive payment of ten thousand bucks. If Hatfield failed, he would receive only enough money to cover his transportation and living expenses.

Hatfield set up shop in early June 1906. Once again he assembled the tall towers and mixed up large batches of his home brew. Hatfield stirred and stirred this magic potion. Boil, boil, toil and trouble. Large clouds of smoke went soaring skyward. Yet, by late July, Hatfield produced barely a drop of rain. In fact, it was one of the driest Julys on record. Alaskan residents grew increasingly impatient with this man. Hatfield was basically driven out of town, but not before he secured about $1,100 to cover his expenses.

One would think that with Hatfield's career ruined this would have been the end of the story, but it was not. Let's face it, no one ever lists all of the jobs that he fails at on his résumé. Many people still believed in Hatfield's abilities and the rainmaking jobs continued to pour (get it?) in.

In December 1915, members of the San Diego Wide Awake Improvement Club approached Hatfield. You know exactly what they wanted—good old H-two-O. It seems that San Diego had built its Morena reservoir back in 1897, but due to low rainfall, it had never come close to reaching capacity. City planners knew that the city's growth hinged on an ample water supply.

Hatfield offered the city a deal with the following stipulations. If he provided less than forty inches of rain, the city would owe him nothing. The city would compensate Hatfield at the rate of $1,000 per inch between forty and fifty inches. Any rainfall above fifty inches would also be free.

The city seemed uninterested in Hatfield's apparent quackery, so he modified the proposal. He offered to fill the reservoir up to capacity for a flat $10,000. If he failed to do so within one year's time, the city would owe him absolutely nothing. With nothing to lose, the city council decided to hire him.

Well, one should be very, very, very, very careful what one asks for.

In early January 1916, Hatfield and his brother Paul did their usual routine of setting up his evaporating tanks on high platforms near the Morena Dam. Within days the clouds rolled in and it started to pour.

And it rained . . .

And rained . . .

And rained . . .

Well, you get the idea.

The sudden downpour flooded the region. Homes and farms were flooded. Roads in and out of the region were under many feet of water. Getting supplies into the city became nearly impossible. The rain stopped on January 20, but the dry spell lasted only a few days.

And it rained . . .

So much water fell from the sky that both the Otay and Sweetwater reservoirs reached capacity and eventually overflowed. On the evening of January 27, 1926, the Lower Otay dam gave way and approximately 13 billion gallons of water rushed down the valley in its journey to the sea. Nearly twenty people (the exact number varies with different sources) were killed by the water's torrent. Houses were swept off their foundations. Railroad service had to be discontinued to the region because long stretches of track had been washed away. All but two of the region's 112 bridges were wiped out. The destruction of telephone and telegraph lines assured a total lack of communication.

Surprisingly, the Hatfield brothers were oblivious to all of the damage that they were causing farther down the valley.

When the rain finally tapered off, the Morena reservoir was within inches of its capacity. They had succeeded in fulfilling their contract.

While dismantling their equipment, the brothers learned that a group of angry farmers was coming after them. Under the assumed name of the Benson brothers, they quickly packed up and fled to San Diego to get their money.

Of course, the city refused to pay Hatfield. It seems that in all the excitement to start his rainmaking process, Charles apparently had never signed the contract. Oops! No contract meant that the city did not have to pay. Hatfield threatened to sue, so

The Sweetwater Dam before Charles Hatfield launched the storm that would ultimately destroy it. (Library of Congress)

the city offered him a deal that he had no choice but to refuse. The city told Hatfield that it would pay him the $10,000 if he agreed to assume all liability for the estimated sixty deaths and $3.5 million in damages caused by the floods. Hatfield wasn't a fool, so he refused their offer and filed suit.

Eventually, two different court decisions ruled that Hatfield's great flood was an act of God. This meant that since Hatfield did not cause the rain, he could receive no compensation for his efforts. One of Hatfield's lawsuits remained on the books until 1938, at which time the courts declared the suit a dead issue.

Hatfield may have been denied payment, but word spread worldwide about his San Diego rainmaking success. Queries for Hatfield's services came from all over the world, although he continued to do the majority of his work in the California region. A 1929 contract involved dousing a raging forest fire in Honduras in a mere ten days. The onset of the depression forced Hatfield to retire from his life as a rainmaker. He settled into the Eagle Rock suburb of Los Angeles and returned to his life as a sewing machine salesman.

During his lifetime, he had claimed to have had caused over five hundred successful rainmaking events. In 1956, Hatfield was invited to attend the Hollywood premiere of the movie *The Rainmaker,* starring Burt Lancaster. (Any guesses who inspired the movie?) When Hatfield died on January 12, 1958, at the age of eighty-two, he took his rainmaking secrets to the grave. I guess that we will never know if he was a real rainmaker or just another quack.

Useless? Useful? I'll leave that for you to decide.

PART 3:

inventive
genius

kitty litter

what's the scoop?

It was a cold day way back in January 1948 that a chance encounter would launch a near billion-dollar-a-year industry. Yes, it was on this day in the village of Cassopolis, Michigan, that a woman named Kay Draper ran into some serious trouble: the sand pile that she used to fill her cat's litter box was frozen solid.

Kay decided to try using ashes in the litter box. She quickly ran into a bigger problem; those little paws produced jet-black paw prints all over her house. Clearly, ashes were not the solution to her problem. So, Kay decided to try sawdust, another popular alternative, in the cat pan. That didn't work well, either. Next, Kay went to visit her neighbors, the Lowes, who operated a coal, ice, and sawdust supply company.

Whoa! Wait a minute. A sawdust supply company? People actually sold this waste product? Let's sidetrack from our story for a moment.

You read it correctly. Sawdust. You may find it hard to believe, but there once was a market for this stuff. They sold it as an industrial absorbent. Spill some grease or oil—drop some sawdust on it to absorb the spill. You get the idea. As you can imagine, sawdust and oil have one major problem—*fire!* So, the Lowes introduced a new absorbent material for these spills—a kiln-dried clay known as Fuller's Earth.

Now we can get back to our story where we find Kay Draper visiting the Lowe facility in search of some sand for her cat's litter box . . .

Here she ran into a twenty-seven-year-old guy named Ed Lowe, who was working for his dad after his stint in the Navy. Ed was trying to expand the family business and had been unsuccessful in trying to convince chicken farmers to use the Fuller's Earth as a nesting material. And, like any good salesman, Ed had his trunk filled with his product.

You know where this story is leading.

Ed couldn't peddle the clay to the chicken farmers, but he somehow convinced Kay that it would make a great cat litter. (Not that he had ever tried it on a cat.)

Edward Lowe's invention of Kitty Litter, shown here in an early photograph, launched an entire industry devoted to cats. (Copyright © 2000 by the Edward Lowe Foundation. Reprinted with permission. All rights reserved.)

Kay shortly returned for more of the clay granules. She recommended the stuff to her friends, and soon they came calling for some Fuller's Earth. Ed had a hunch that he might be on to something big. He filled ten paper bags with the stuff and labeled them with a grease pencil—you guessed it—Kitty Litter.

The stuff was not an overnight success, however. The initial five-pound bags sold for sixty-five cents, but no one would buy them. Ed told the local pet store owner to give the bags away, which he did. Once the customers saw how wonderful the product was, they were actually willing to pay money for the stuff.

Ed traveled the country attending cat shows and visiting pet shops in an attempt to move the product. Cat owners eventually fell in love with the product, and the rest is cat litter history.

A private investment group, collectively known as Golden Cat, purchased Ed's company for over $200 million plus stock options in 1990. Ed retired and used part of his fortune to establish the Edward Lowe Foundation to help other entrepreneurs. Sadly, Ed Lowe passed away on October 4, 1995.

The success of Kitty Litter enabled pet owners to keep cats inside their homes with little muss or fuss (let's not discuss smell). As a result, an entire industry consisting of cat foods, toys, grooming products, and the like was launched.

Today, the traditional clay cat litter that Ed Lowe introduced still commands the lion's share of the market at approximately 55 percent.

Catching up with 40 percent of sales is clumping litter. Clumping litter is made from clays such as sodium bentonite or attapulgus (it was originally found in Attapulgus, Georgia). These special clays bond well with a cat's waste and form hard clumps that can be easily removed from the litter box.

The remainder of the litter market is made up of a very wide variety of products. Pretty much anything goes here. They use silica gel beads, cedar chips, pelletized newspaper, peels from citrus fruits, peanut hulls, corncobs, and semolina wheat. (Maybe someone can figure out how to use all of our tossed-out nonabsorbent plastic.)

What started out as a pile of nesting material has turned into an estimated 2.5 billion-pound, three-quarters-of a-billion-dollar industry that even has its own Washington lobbyist.

Now you know the scoop.

Useless? Useful? I'll leave that for you to decide.

einstein's refrigerator

he really did design modern iceboxes

Einstein.

It's amazing how many images that one simple name brings to mind. Genius. Scientist. Theory of relativity. $E=mc^2$. Messy hair.

Yet, what few people know is that Einstein actually spent a number of years inventing refrigerators. And this occurred years *after* he became the most famous scientist in the world.

So, you're probably sitting there wondering why a man with a Nobel Prize, worldwide fame, and genius intellect would stoop so low as to waste his time working on such a mundane project as refrigerators.

Well, to Einstein this seemed like a very important project. According to most accounts, Einstein was sitting in Germany one day in the early 1920s and came across a newspaper article that described the death of an entire family—a mother, father, and their children. Apparently, they had been killed in their sleep by a poisonous coolant that had leaked out of their refrigerator.

Keep in mind that most people still had iceboxes at this time. Newfangled mechanical refrigerators were starting to gain popularity, but as the brief news story above attests, they could be very dangerous. All of the coolants available in the early days of refrigeration (ammonia, sulfur dioxide, and methyl chloride) were very toxic and would kill if they leaked out into the home.

Einstein knew that there had to be a better way. (At this point I see images of Einstein throwing on his Super Genius uniform and flying to the rescue in a Superman-like fashion.)

Enter into the picture a guy named Leo Szilard. Szilard is considered by many to be the father of the nuclear age, but he was just starting his career at this time. He was the person who envisioned the nuclear chain reaction that could be used to generate massive amounts of power (apparently the No Nukes movement had not taken hold that early in the century). Szilard later realized that the chain reaction could be used to build weapons of mass destruction and urged Einstein to write that now famous letter to President Roosevelt (the one that was the catalyst for the whole Manhattan Project).

The two great scientific minds came together and concluded that the problem with refrigeration was not just limited to the poisonous coolant. The fact that refrigerators were mechanical in nature was the real culprit. Anyone with even the slightest mechanical experience knows that moving parts cause wear and tear on any system. Eliminate the moving parts and the system will probably never leak.

As great physicists, the men realized that they could use their knowledge of thermodynamics to produce a cooling system that did not involve any type of mechanical motion.

Einstein and Szilard came up with many different designs, but decided to focus on the three most promising concepts. While modern refrigeration utilizes mechanical compressors, the scientists conceptualized refrigerators that depended on three totally independent scientific principles: that of electromagnetism, absorption, and diffusion. Let's not forget that all of their designs contained no moving parts.

In early 1926, Szilard filed the first of many patents that the two men would share. Since Einstein had spent so many of his early years working in the Swiss Patent Office, they were able to prepare the patent applications without the help of expensive lawyers.

Of course, a patent is nice, but earning $$$ is even better. That same year, Szilard also negotiated a contract with the German company Bamag-Meguin. Unfortunately, the deal fell through less than a year later when the company ran into financial difficulties and was forced to drop many questionable research projects.

With a name like Einstein, one would guess that it wouldn't be difficult to find another manufacturer to pick up the project. Within a few short months, the two scientists were able to sign contracts with the Swedish firm AB Electrolux and the German A.E.G. (essentially the German General Electric Company). AB Electrolux paid Einstein and Szilard approximately $750 for their patents (about $10,000 in turn-of-the-millennium funds). Yet, the company never developed the refrigeration concepts any further. In typical corporate fashion, the patents were purchased by Electrolux simply to eliminate any competition to their own designs.

The A.E.G. (which stands for Allgemeine Elektrizitats Gesellschaft, just in case you needed to know), however, decided to develop what later became known as the Einstein-Szilard electromagnetic pump for use in a refrigerator.

DANGER! WILL ROBINSON. DANGER!

TECHNICAL INFORMATION AHEAD!

In the simplest of terms, the induction pump worked something like this. A liquid metal was sealed in a welded stainless steel container. Coils of wire wrapped around the cylinder, which allowed the electromagnetic field surrounding the liquid to be varied. And, as any high school physics student knows (at least he or she should know!), a metal that is placed in a varying electromagnetic field will move at a right angle to the field. In other words, the liquid metal ends up being pumped without ever contacting the current. The moving liquid metal acted like a piston that compressed the refrigerant. Heat was released by an array of condenser coils like those found on the back of modern refrigerators.

END OF WARNING!

THIS HAS BEEN A SERVICE OF THE PUBLIC TECHNOLOGY WARNING SYSTEM.

Back to our story:

On July 31, 1931, the Einstein-Szilard refrigerator went into continuous operation. It worked like a charm, although it was very noisy.

So what happened to the Einstein-Szilard refrigerator?

The whole project was dropped for a number of reasons. The worldwide depression certainly didn't help things. Nor did continual improvements in refrigerator design. But the 1930 invention of Freon was the real killer of the Einstein-Szilard refrigerator. Freon was a nontoxic refrigerant, so the danger of leaking was eliminated. There was no longer a need to redesign the refrigerator.

Oddly, that was not really the end of the Einstein-Szilard system, however. The pump was later incorporated into the cooling systems of nuclear breeder reactors.

In the end, the two great scientists filed more than forty-five patents in six countries. The contributions of these great minds to the field of refrigeration is largely forgotten, but their other achievements will long be considered among the greatest of the twentieth century.

Useless? Useful? I'll leave that for you to decide.

the foot thingy

whatchamacallit?

He used it. She used it. They've all used it. In fact, we can be pretty sure that even you have used it. And not just once. Yes, even I am willing to admit that I've used it.

What we are dealing with here is the most universally accepted measuring device on the North American continent.

You're probably guessing that I'm talking about a ruler, but I'm not. We've all used rulers, but there is certainly no standard ruler design. (They are not even all straight.)

This universally adopted device that I'm talking about is that contraption that the shoe salesguy (or gal) sticks your foot into to measure the size of your foot.

You know what I'm talking about. It's that really cold metal thing with all the markings on it that you put your foot in.

All-metal construction gives it some really nice heft. (There must be a few bratty kids out there who have cracked their siblings' skulls open with this thing.) Come to think of it, this gizmo is probably the only thing in America that hasn't been redesigned into a cheap designer plastic imitation.

So, do you have any idea what this device is called? Few people outside the shoe industry do. Yet, the name is printed as clear as day on the top of the device, although your foot obscures the name when you actually use it.

This device is called (drum roll, please!):

The Brannock Device.

The Brannock Device was patented in 1927 by a Syracuse University student named Charles F. Brannock. (Big surprise on the name, huh?) At the time, Brannock's dad Otis was a partner in the Park-Brannock shoe store located in downtown Syracuse. The younger Brannock realized that there was a big problem. To measure a customer for a proper fit, the salesmen had just two options: Use either a crude wooden measuring stick or just keep trying on shoes until the proper fit was achieved. Brannock knew that there had to be a better way and spent endless sleepless nights solving the problem. His original prototype was made from one of those childhood Erector sets and the rest is shoe history.

Just in case you're curious, the size system is linear. For example, a men's size 1 is $7\,{}^{2}/_{3}$ inches. Each additional size is ${}^{1}/_{3}$ inch longer.

Widths work the same way. Each width is separated by a distance of ${}^{3}/_{16}$ of an inch. There are actually nine widths in the U.S. system (width actually varies with foot length): AAA, AA, A, B, C, D, E, EE, and EEE.

Today, the Brannock Device is the standard for the footwear industry.

If you think about it, the Brannock Device has one other distinct honor; it's one of the few things that you can just throw on the floor anywhere and it looks fine. Throw a shoe, a piece of paper, or anything else on the floor and it's considered a mess. Not so with the Brannock Device. It belongs on the floor.

You can't kill one of these things, either. They are essentially indestructible, although I am sure that any good explosion could destroy it. I have noticed that the numbers do eventually wear away with use, but there are many stores out there that have been using the same device for thirty or forty years. (If only my car could last this long.)

Even with the great success of his foot-measuring device,

Charles Brannock continued to operate his shoe store until 1981 when his building was sold to allow for the expansion of the Hotel Syracuse. Sadly, Charles Brannock died in 1993 at the age of eighty-nine.

The company has since been purchased by Sal Leonardi (do you know him?), who owned a small tool factory and just happened to be looking to acquire a new product line. With approximately 1 million devices sold, the Brannock Device has varied very little, although the company has started manufacturing customized models and is currently considering producing a digital model.

So, the next time you're in the mall and you want to impress your friends, just drag them into any shoe store. Point to that metal measuring device sitting on the floor and show them your brilliance. That, my friend, is a Brannock Device . . .

Side note: Being a member of the EEE club, it is clear that I have really fat feet. I guess that I won't be doing much foot modeling in the near future. My friend Brett, on the other hand, has great-looking feet. Years ago, while he was sunbathing at college, some stranger came up to him and told him that he had really beautiful feet. The guy ended up shooting tons of pictures of Brett's feet. Yes, there are some really strange people in this world!

Useless? Useful? I'll leave that for you to decide.

america's first subway

it was one big secret

Most major cities around the world have been faced at some time in history with the question of what to do with all the traffic in the streets. Today, those smelly buses and graffiti-covered trains have been providing a somewhat viable solution. But what happened when cities were faced with this problem during the 1800s?

Imagine what it must have been like in a large city back in the nineteenth century. There were millions of people with no practical means of mass transportation. Remember, engine-powered vehicles practical for city use had not been invented yet. Just tons of horse-drawn carriages creating one stinky mess in the city streets. Hold your nose!

Such a transportation problem existed in New York City and, to no one's surprise, there was no practical solution.

Enter one Alfred Ely Beach. Don't worry if you don't know who this guy is—most people don't.

What you do need to know is that in 1846 Alfred purchased a newly launched publication called *The Scientific American* with a friend named Orsun D. Munn. He quickly became its editor and turned it into the great magazine that we know today (although they seem to have dropped the *The* from their name).

You're probably wondering where he got the cash to purchase this great magazine. Since you just had to know, I will tell you.

Beach got his start working for the *New York Sun*, the city's first penny daily newspaper. It would be nice to say that he had to work his way up through the ranks, but he didn't. You see, his father owned the paper. By 1848, management was turned over to Alfred and his brother Moses.

So here we have young Alfred in charge of both a great scientific magazine and a leading newspaper. Day after day he glanced out the window of his lofty *Sun* office to the congested city streets below. Just horse-and-buggy gridlock (better watch where you step!). Surely, he wondered, there must be a solution to this problem. Well, he actually came up with two solutions.

The first was to build elevated roads and place the extra traffic above. Very costly and not very practical.

The second possibility was to go underground. In 1849, he proposed to tunnel the entire length of Broadway and put down a double track. But this was not a track for trains—it was for horses. One track for each direction. Horses pulling cars behind them would stop at every corner for ten seconds and then move on down the track. But such a far-fetched scheme was not to happen. At least not yet.

Beach moved on to bigger and better things.

You see, Beach and Munn had also opened a patent agency in 1846 called Munn & Co. (Al was one busy guy). This was no small-time operation. Many important inventors walked through their doors. Some guy named Thomas Edison demonstrated his newfangled contraption called a phonograph for the first time ever to Beach. Other important inventors like Alexander Graham Bell and Samuel Morse also sought out the company's assistance. Between 1850 and 1860, Beach commuted from New York to Washington every two weeks to look over his clients' affairs.

Oh, yeah. As if Beach wasn't busy enough, he also invented some of his own things. In 1856, he won First Prize and a gold medal at New York's Crystal Palace Exhibition. Beach had invented a typewriter for the blind that moved the paper carriage along with every keystroke. This mechanism was eventually adopted for use in all standard typewriters.

During the same period, Beach turned total control of the *Sun* over to his brother and in 1853 started a new publication called the *People's Journal.*

Busy guy.

But Beach never lost sight of the traffic problem that faced the city. The population of New York City was growing and growing. More people meant crowded streets, unsanitary conditions, and more horses racing up and down the city's thoroughfares (actually they spent most of their time standing still in traffic).

In March 1864, a man named Hugh B. Wilson offered a solution to the traffic problem. Wilson was a Michigan railroad man and financier and had attended the opening of the London subway in January 1863. What was good for London must be good for New York. Unfortunately, the proposed bill was defeated. Why? Very simple—Boss Tweed, who headed the city Tammany Hall political machine, received a kickback on every fare in the city. Allowing a subway to be built would cause a loss of revenue. Tweed controlled the governor's office and this bill was dead in the water before it was ever proposed.

Even if the bill had passed, the idea would never have been a success.

The London steam locomotives burned coke and stored the exhaust in special tanks mounted below the boilers. Unfortunately, they didn't work properly. The passengers were forced to store the smoke in their lungs, if you know what I mean. More than one person died from this exhaust.

In other words, locomotives were out. Electric motors had not been perfected yet and subways seemed to be an impossibility.

But wait! We forgot about Alfred Beach!

Beach still had his mind set on doing something about that awful traffic congestion.

Through his various contacts, Beach learned of a pneumatic mail tube that had been successfully built in London in 1866. You've probably seen small versions of these devices at your bank's drive-through teller. You put your transaction into a little container, close the hatch, and air pressure sends it on its way into the bank building. Whoooosh!

The British tube was four and a half feet high and two miles in length. Its sole purpose was to quickly move mail and packages from one place to another. As you are probably well aware, humans tend to do idiotic things. Scrunching down and going for a ride on one of the mail carriers just happened to be one of them.

Beach quickly realized that if the concept was enlarged to carry packages of humans, all of the city's transit problems would be gone. He was convinced that pneumatic transit was the solution and decided to give it a shot.

In 1867, Beach unveiled his idea to the world at the American Institute Fair being held at the Fourteenth Street Armory in New York. His model consisted of a tube six feet in diameter. The walls of the tube were one and one half inches thick, made of fifteen layers of wood laminated together. The tube was suspended from the roof of the building and ran 107 feet from Fourteenth Street to Fifteenth Street. The car, which ran on wheels and was confined to a track, was moved back and forth by a ten-foot-diameter fan. The ten-passenger car was kept in constant motion and was a smash hit. More than 170,000 people took a ride on this model before the close of the exhibition. To no one's surprise, Beach took home the Gold Medal for his invention.

Translating this successful prototype into reality would not be easy. Tunnel drilling equipment just didn't exist at the time and Boss Tweed still controlled the political scene. Beach knew that in order to build his proposed subway he would need to obtain a city franchise. But to do so would probably mean funneling hundreds of thousands of dollars into Tweed's pockets.

Building the subway in secret was the only solution. Beach formed a company called the Pneumatic Dispatch Company and proposed to tunnel two tubes, each four and one half feet in diameter and approximately one-half mile in length. These tubes were intended to carry packages under Broadway between Warren Street and Cedar Street. Since the tubes would only carry mail, Tweed did not object and the project was easily approved. In fact, Tweed had expected Beach to propose a pneumatic elevated train and was very happy to see Beach's focus diverted. A charter was issued to Beach.

An engraving of a passenger riding in Beach's luxurious subway car. (*Scientific American*, March 5, 1870)

Then Beach pulled a fast one. He went back to the legislature and requested an amendment to the legislation. He said that he wanted one large tube in order to simplify construction and save money. This very minor change easily passed.

I bet you can now see where this story is going.

Beach wasted no time and did everything possible to keep his project a secret. His first move was to rent the basement of Devlin's Clothing Store, which was located at the corner of Broadway and Warren Street.

To cut the tunnel, Beach invented a hydraulic shield that could gouge out sixteen inches of earth with each advance. Six people operated the machine: two to work the hydraulic rams, two to carry out the earth, and two to put in the tunnel's brickwork.

All work on the tunnel was done at night.

Why nights?

Very simple. Trying to build a secret tunnel in the middle of a major city was virtually impossible during the day. All the work on the tunnel was done at night in an effort to minimize public attention. Bags of soil were also smuggled out and taken away on covered wagons with muffled wheels.

The tunnel was drilled at approximately 21 feet below street level. The soil proved to be fairly soft. The only obstacle encountered was the foundation of an old fort, but the shield was able to go through it without any problem. The entire 312-foot tube was dug out in just fifty-eight nights.

Then, when the subway was nearly complete, a reporter disguised as a workman gained access to the tunnel. As a result, the *New York Herald* revealed Beach's secret to the world. The newspaper's description was fairly accurate and critically attacked the feasibility of such a project.

Beach counteracted. He opened his tunnel for all to see on February 28, 1870. He charged 25 cents admission and people were shocked to see what was hidden in the ground below.

Upon entering the rented store at street level, visitors descended a flight of stairs to Beach's masterpiece. He spared no expense. He knew that he had to use this tunnel to impress even the harshest of critics.

The subway waiting room was 120 feet long and 14 feet wide. It was brightly lit with zircon lamps. There was a cascading fountain filled with goldfish that helped to muffle the sound of the street traffic above. Frescoes, fancy chandeliers, and blind windows (with damask curtains) lined the walls. Let's not forget the grandfather clock and the grand piano. This was clearly not your typical subway. (Today everything would be stolen or vandalized within the first twenty-four hours.)

Spectators descended six more steps down to the train platform where the tunnel came into view. There it was, engraved in the tunnel's header: PNEUMATIC (1870) SUBWAY. On either side of the tunnel entrance was a bronze statue of Mercury holding a cluster of red, green, and blue gaslights. Mercury was an appropriate choice, as he was the messenger of the gods, the symbol of the great speed of the winds.

The subway car was equally lavish. It was very brightly lit by gaslights and furnished with cushioned seats that could accommodate twenty-two passengers at a time.

When the doors to the car closed, a giant fan (called the Western Tornado) kicked into action and pushed the car along the track at six miles per hour, although it was capable of going much faster.

Oh, I almost forgot. So that Beach would not break his charter, there was a thousand-foot eight-inch diameter mail dispatch tube incorporated into the tunnel. It carried packages at about sixty miles per hour from a drop box hidden in a hollow lamppost on the street above.

The cost of the tunnel project was about $350,000, including approximately $70,000 of Beach's own money.

The pneumatic subway was an instant smash. Very quickly, the *New York Herald* changed its opinion and now called for the building of a pneumatic subway that went to every corner of the city.

Obviously, this never happened.

Why?

Boss Tweed, again, stood in the way. A bill to extend Beach's subway five miles to Central Park passed both houses of the legislature by a wide margin. But good old Boss Tweed ordered then-Governor John T. Hoffman to veto the bill. Beach tried again in 1873 after Tweed and his cronies were toppled from power. This time there was a new governor, John A. Dix, and the bill was signed into law.

But luck was not on Beach's side. Just a few weeks after the bill was passed, the financial panic of 1873 set in. People had bigger concerns than worrying about building a subway.

Yes, the pneumatic subway was dead and buried.

Beach allowed the subway tunnel to be used as a shooting gallery and later as a wine cellar, but he never was able to clear a profit. Giving up, Beach had the tunnel sealed and it was forgotten.

Beach died in 1896 without ever seeing a subway built in New York City.

Of course, one was eventually built. In February 1912, when the Degnon Contracting Company was constructing part of the new Broadway subway tunnel, they cut right into Beach's old pneumatic tube. The construction workers actually knew that the subway was there, so it was no great surprise when they found it.

However, they were shocked to see how intact the entire pneumatic subway was. The tunnel and its accompanying station were in great shape. The car still sat on the tracks, although most of its wood components had rotted away. The hydraulic shield still sat there waiting to complete Beach's dream.

Today, a discovery of this type would be preserved. Unfortunately, this did not happen in 1912. The old subway tunnel was excavated and made part of the new BMT City Hall subway station. No one knows for sure, but it is believed that the pneumatic subway station itself is still intact and buried somewhere under the city's streets.

In 1940, a bronze plaque to commemorate Beach and his creation was erected in the subway station. Don't try to find it today—it disappeared from the walls of the station years ago. (It probably has been replaced by graffiti.)

Beach is another one of those great thinkers whom history has forgotten. This seems to be the typical honor for those who are ahead of their time.

Interesting side note: Take a visit to any one of the thousands of Subway sandwich shops around the world and you will see images of Beach's pneumatic subway incorporated into the wallpaper.

Useless? Useful? I'll leave that for you to decide.

vaseline

it's yummy for your tummy!

This story is a favorite among people whom I have told it to.

After all, we know Vaseline is Mmm, mmm, good!

First, a bit about where this multipurpose goop comes from:

It all started way back in 1859 in Brooklyn, New York. Imagine a young chemist named Robert Chesebrough (of Chesebrough-Ponds fame) at work in his office. Young Robby was burdened by a very common problem of the time: He sold kerosene for fuel, but the great oil strikes in Pennsylvania threatened his livelihood. It was clear to him that oil was to become the fuel source of the future.

What to do? What to do?

He did the obvious thing. He hopped in his horse and buggy and made his way to Titusville, Pennsylvania, the home of the oil well. His intention was to strike it rich in the oil industry.

However, he became intrigued with a paraffin-like gooey substance that stuck to the drilling rigs. The riggers hated this stuff because it caused the drilling rigs to seize up. For all the problems this substance caused, the riggers found one small use. When they rubbed it on a cut or bruise it sped healing.

Robby bottled the stuff up and dragged it back to his Brooklyn laboratory. It didn't take him long to extract the key pasty ingredient, the translucent material we now know as petroleum jelly. He received his patent for the wonder jelly in 1870.

He needed a guinea pig to test it out on. Slashing his wife and kids up for the sake of science was definitely out of the question. He chose to inflict all types of cuts and burns on himself to test the stuff out. The injuries all seemed to heal quickly without any sign of infection when the goop was applied.

His next problem: what to name it?

We can imagine the names he may have tossed around—"Yellow slippery stuff," "100-million-year-old stuff from oil wells," or "Slip 'n Slide brand lubricant."

They were all catchy names for our modern society, but people were dumber back then (your parents were dumber than you and they thought the same of their parents, and so on . . .).

He chose a great name—Vaseline.

Why Vaseline? No one really knows.

I like to believe the story that he stored the stuff in his wife's vases in the lab, and since all medical products back then ended in "ine" (Listerine, Murine, etc.)—he came up with Vaseline. Others claim that it is derived from the Greek words *wasser* (water) and *elain* (oil). You can choose whichever version you like better. (Or, you could make up your own. No one would be any the wiser.)

Selling it was easy for Chesebrough. He simply loaded up his horse and buggy and gave out free samples across New York State. Within six months he had twelve buggy setups distributing the stuff.

People used this goop for everything: cuts and bruises, removing stains from furniture, polishing wood surfaces, restoring leather, preventing rust, cat hairball remedy, and as a sexual aid (you can use your imagination on this one). Druggists used Vaseline as a base for their other medicines and ointments.

It is very safe to assume that Mr. Chesebrough (we can't possibly refer to him as Robby anymore) was a very wealthy man. In 1881, the company came under the control of Standard

Oil. In May 1909, at the age of seventy-two, Chesebrough was forced to give up the presidency of the company under Standard's mandatory retirement rule.

The best use of Vaseline ever had to be by Mr. Chesebrough himself. He believed that a person should *eat a spoonful every day for good health.*

He lived to ninety-six years of age and never missed that delicious spoonful every morning.

Too bad he ate the goop; he probably would have lived until 106 years of age if he hadn't gulped that stuff down!

Useless? Useful? I'll leave that for you to decide.

(Vaseline is a registered trademark of Chesebrough-Ponds, Inc.)

hedy lamarr

not exactly your typical nerdy inventor with a pocket protector

Hedy Lamarr is best known as the incredibly beautiful and sexy screen siren of the World War II era. In modern *Wayne's World* speak, she was babelicious. Yet, perhaps the most fascinating part of Lamarr's life had absolutely nothing to do with her beauty or film career. Hedy Lamarr is almost certainly the only Hollywood star who has claim to a patent on a significant technological breakthrough—one that has become the basis for modern communications.

Lamarr was frequently quoted as saying, "Any girl can be glamorous. All you have to do is stand still and look stupid." She may have played that role on the silver screen, but when it came to real life, Hedy proved that brainpower was everything.

Before examining her important contribution, let's take a quick look at her background (in case your memory has failed you, or, as in my case, you are too young to have ever known):

First of all, Lamarr was only her stage name. She was actually born Hedwig Eva Maria Kiesler in Vienna, Austria, on November 9, 1913.

As a teenager, Hedy attended acting school and quickly made the transition into films. Like most movie stars, her first few films were forgettable. Yet, the one that she made at age seventeen made her an international star. A very controversial star, that is. In the Czech film *Ecstasy*, Lamarr acted in a steamy love scene and appeared nude in a ten-minute swimming sequence. That was definitely not the thing to do. While mild by today's standards, her nudity was considered morally unacceptable at the time, and the film was banned in the United States for several years on charges of indecency.

In 1933, at age nineteen, her parents placed her in an arranged marriage with an Austrian armament manufacturer named Fritz Mandl. Mandl was the type of shady character who would sell arms to anyone, even if it meant selling them in violation of the Versailles Treaty.

Of course, to make these deals, Mandl had to entertain all of his prospects. This included attending hundreds of dinners with the likes of Hitler and Mussolini. And what would a business dinner be like without Mandl's gorgeous and equally famous wife dazzling these arms developers, buyers, and manufacturers? But as we will soon learn from the outcome of this story, Hedy did not just entertain these men. She listened carefully and learned a great deal.

To an outsider, Hedy had everything. She was married to one of the wealthiest men in Europe. She lived in the famous Salzburg castle where *The Sound of Music* was filmed. Add to that all the clothes, jewelry, servants, and cars (one 1935 Mercedes owned by Mandl sold for over $200,000 several years ago) one could ever want. It sure sounds like the ideal life to me, but it was not.

Hedy became more of a trophy than a wife to Mandl. He was a control freak and would not even let her go swimming without his supervision. After four years of marriage, Hedy could take no more. She decided to escape.

In her first attempt to flee, Mandl followed her. She was forced to sneak into a club that had peep shows upstairs. Hedy paid off the attendant to keep his mouth shut, but Mandl paid even more to get in. Hedy was forced to hide in one of the rooms. While she was in there, a male customer came in and assumed that Hedy was the lady he had hired to spend the evening with him. Without going into all of the details, Hedy was forced into the position of having sex with the man to avoid her husband (she claimed that he was banging on the door).

During her real escape, Hedy supposedly drugged (that old trick—three sleeping pills in the coffee) the maid that was assigned to her, put on a maid's uniform, and walked out the service entrance to freedom. Hedy eventually made it to London, where she appeared on the stage.

Hedy hopped aboard the ship *Normandie* bound for Hollywood and stardom. She signed a contract with MGM's Louis B. Mayer while on the boat, but he insisted on a name change to avoid the controversy from *Ecstasy*. At this point, MGM publicist Howard Strickling (according to a 1970 *New York Times* article) approached Hedy and handed her a typewritten list of last names and asked her to make a choice. You guessed it; she chose Lamarr and the rest is Hollywood history. Lamarr was immediately crowned the most beautiful woman in the world by MGM and quickly became one of Hollywood's glamour gals.

Which leads us to the real focus of this story: her incredible invention.

First, I must introduce you to the other lead character in this story, George Antheil. Antheil was internationally famous for his mechanistic avant-garde musical style. When Antheil moved to Hollywood, he became a film composer and a syndicated columnist for *Esquire* magazine, to which he also contributed articles on romance and endocrinology. He even published a book on the subject—the 1937 *Every Man His Own Detective: A Study of Glandular Endocrinology*. What made him an expert on this subject one will never know. Maybe it is because, according to my hormone-laden teenage students, that if you say "pianist" very quickly, it sounds just like "penis." Since they sound so much alike, one can only conclude that being an expert in the first makes one knowledgeable in the latter. (Well, maybe I am stretching it a wee bit here . . .)

In the summer of 1940, Lamarr sought out Antheil. They were neighbors in Hollywood and supposedly met at a party. The story goes that Hedy did not want to see Antheil about his music. Lamarr wanted to consult Antheil about glands— her mammary glands to be specific. Lamarr wanted to find out how she could enlarge the size of her breasts. (Doesn't this part of the story seem kind of fishy? Only two articles actually make this claim.)

Very quickly, it became clear that Antheil didn't have the answer (those toxic silicone implants had not been invented yet), so the topic of

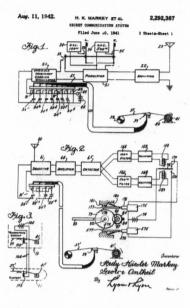

Hedy Lamarr's and George Antheil's patent for their Secret Communication System.

conversation changed to the impending war and torpedoes. Lamarr feared Hitler (remember that she actually knew the guy) and began to talk about an idea that she had for the radio control of torpedoes. At the time, radio control sounded like a great idea, but was not practical. All one had to do was jam the particular frequency that the torpedo operated on and the missile would fail to reach its target.

Lamarr was sitting at the piano with Antheil when that flash of genius struck her. Antheil was hitting keys on the piano and she would repeat the sequence. It became clear that Antheil was changing the keys that he was hitting, yet he was still able to communicate to her. What if this could be translated into radio control for a torpedo?

The next day they sat on his floor and figured the whole scheme out. Lamarr realized that the frequency needed to be randomly changed so that the enemy could not jam it. Any attempt to knock out the signal controlling the missile would only knock out a small blip of the communication stream and have virtually no effect on its overall control. Hence, the concept known as "frequency hopping" was born.

Of course, getting this grand scheme to actually work was another story. Keep in mind that this was the time of large vacuum tubes, not the miniaturized microprocessors that rule our world today.

Antheil offered the solution to the problem. He had previously composed his *Ballet mechanique,* which was scored for sixteen player pianos to perform at the same time. He suggested using punched piano rolls to keep the radio transmitter and torpedo receiver in synch. The transmitting signal was designed to broadcast over a band of eighty-eight possible frequencies, one for each key of the piano keyboard.

It took Lamarr and Antheil several months to work out the exact details of their invention. Then, in December of 1940, they sent a description of their idea to the National Inventor's Council (set up by the government to get ideas from the general public). Very few of the hundreds of thousands of submissions that the council ever received actually caused any kind of excitement, but Lamarr's and Antheil's did. Under the direction of the council's chairman (and inventive bigwig over at General Motors), Charles Kettering, the government helped to improve the concept. Patent 2,292,387 for the "Secret Communication System" was granted on August 11, 1942. (The patent is actually under her married name at the time—Hedy Kiesler Markey.)

Unfortunately, other members of the council were less than enthusiastic. There's no surprise here—just think about the feasibility of placing a synchronized player piano mechanism into a torpedo and having it operate properly. The Navy declared the mechanism too cumbersome and shelved the idea. The concept of frequency hopping was too far ahead of its time. Lamarr and Antheil pursued their invention no further.

Yet, Lamarr was still able to help out in another way—by selling war bonds. As part of one promotion, anyone who purchased $25,000 worth of bonds could get a kiss from Lamarr (Would Pamela Anderson do the same today?). She was actually able to sell $7 million worth in one night.

Not all great ideas are forgotten, however. In 1957, engineers at the Sylvania Electronics Systems Division, located in Buffalo, New York, used transistor electronics to accomplish the goal that Lamarr and Antheil had set out to achieve years before. Finally, in 1962 (three years after the Lamarr/Antheil patent expired), the concept of frequency hopping was used by the United States government in the communication systems placed aboard ships sent out to blockade Cuba.

Today, the concept is not only used by the military (it is used in the Milstar defense communications satellite system), but it has also become the technology behind the latest in wireless Internet transmission and the newest cellular phones. A quick search of the United States Patent Office shows 1,203 patents dealing with frequency shifting (now called "spread spectrum") between 1995 and 1997. How much influence the Lamarr-Antheil patent has had, if any, on this technology will probably never be known.

Lamarr never earned a penny from this invention from which so many others have profited. Instead, she slowly faded from public view. She was married and divorced six times between 1933 and 1965 to Fritz Mandl, Gene Markey, Sir John Loder, Ted Stauffer, W. Howard Lee (who later married actress Gene Tierney), and Lewis J. Boles. In 1966, Lamarr made international headlines when she was arrested for shoplifting in a May department store in Los Angeles, but was acquitted by a 10–2 jury vote. The bad publicity from this incident coupled with her controversial autobiography, *Ecstasy and Me* (which she later claimed was ghost-written), brought an end to her movie career.

On March 12, 1997, Hedy Lamarr was finally honored by the Electronic Frontier Foundation for her great contribution to society. Her son Anthony Loder accepted the award for his mother and played an audiotape for the audience—the first time she had publicly spoken in over two decades.

Sadly, Hedy Lamarr passed away on January 19, 2000, at her Altamonte Springs home in Florida. The bulk of her nearly $3 million estate was willed to her two children, but a portion was left to her former personal secretary and to a friend. Most surprisingly, however, was that she bequeathed $83,000 to a local police officer who had befriended her in the last years of her life. Lamarr asked that her ashes be scattered over the Vienna Woods, near where she was born in Austria.

In one of those weird twists of fate, that same son Anthony today owns a Los Angeles phone store in which half of the phone systems that he sells are based on his mom's pioneering technology.

Useful? Useless? I'll leave that for you to decide.

the zipper

hey! your fly is open!

Several years ago I posted a short story on the Internet detailing the invention of that thing that holds your fly closed: the zipper. The large volume of e-mail that this story has generated over the years shocked me. Even more surprising was that the bulk of these messages were from students who were writing term papers on the zipper.

I can't help but wonder why students would choose the zipper as their topic. I like to imagine that it goes something like this:

A teacher assigns the student a research paper on any topic of his or her choice. The student is clueless. (We've all been in this boat before.) The student looks down and sees the zipper sitting in his lap below.

Eureka! (A light bulb goes off in the student's head.) The student mumbles something like, "I'll do my report on the zipper!"

That sounds great, but the student has one big problem: Where does one find information on the history of the zipper? To no one's surprise, there is not a whole lot of information out there on this topic. Students almost invariably end up reading my story. (If they are typical, they probably just cut and paste my story into their word processor and put their name at the top.)

In reality, the students have chosen a topic with a fantastic history. It may be hard to believe, but anyone who had seen a zipper during its first thirty years of existence would have been certain that the product was headed straight for obscurity. Yes, the zipper was once a complete and utter failure.

So, where did this great invention come from?

It turns out that the zipper was patented way back on August 29, 1893 (remember that date—it may show up on the exam I'm giving you next week), by a guy named Whitcomb Judson, a Chicago mechanical engineer who received nearly thirty other patents in his lifetime. It basically was a bunch of hooks that were mechanically locked in place by a removable slide. I should mention here that Judson only intended the device to fasten shoes. (Which just happens to be one of the very few places that we rarely use zippers today.) Also, it was not called a zipper; it was simply referred to as the fastener (quite catchy, huh?).

There was one big problem with the zipper—excuse me, the fastener—it just didn't work. Not only did it not work, no one wanted it, either. With a potential audience of 20 million people, Judson decided to display it at the 1893 Chicago World's Fair. With an audience of that size, one would think that he was sure to make a killing.

So, how many did he sell? Was it a hundred thousand? A million?

No, just twenty. Certainly not enough to retire on. All twenty fasteners went to the U.S. Postal Service to close its mailbags. Since it never ordered another batch from Judson, it is safe to assume that the Postal Service was not happy with the product.

By the tenth anniversary of this gadget, there was basically nothing to distinguish it from a host of other crazy schemes and inventions that had failed. As a result, Judson focused his energies on automobiles at the turn of the century, making occasional design changes to the fastener. The zipper was never to make him a rich man, although his son did make millions off one of his dad's automobile patents.

It turns out that Judson's final patent introduced the idea of clamping each of the fastening elements directly to the cloth. His company, Universal Fastener, finally had a fastener that could be manufactured and sold. In 1905, they introduced the *C-Curity* fastener, which was anything but secure. All any woman had to do was bend over and the fastener would pop open. It also didn't help that these fasteners were very expensive to produce and that they were made of steel that rusted when laundered. Believe it or not, the company actually recommended that the fastener be removed every time the clothing was washed! (Just how does one go about doing this?)

It may seem obvious to us today, but people couldn't figure out how to use the zipper. It actually came with a set of directions! (Something like "Make sure your private parts are not hanging out and pull up"?)

Yes, it looked like the zipper was never to be . . .

But wait! The story can't be over. There are zippers here, there, and everywhere.

The saga continues . . .

In 1906, the company hired a German-trained, Swiss-born engineer named Gideon Sundback. Sundback had emigrated to the United States just a year earlier to work for the industrial giant Westinghouse. He later quit in favor of working for the struggling fastener company. You're probably sitting there wondering why anyone would give up such a secure job to go work for a company that was about to fall into financial ruin. The answer was that he apparently did it for love. He was smitten with Elvira Aronson, the daughter of Universal Fastener's main machine designer.

Sundback's first redesign, dubbed the *Plako,* was introduced in 1908. Although an improvement of Judson's final design, the new fastener suffered from many of the same inherent problems of the old model. It was a poor product, but it managed to keep the company in business.

Sundback knew that there had to be a better way. In 1917, Sundback patented a rustproof fastener that lacked the mechanical hooks that had proven to be such a big problem in Judson's original model. Originally called the Hookless Hooker (Sounds a bit dirty, doesn't it?), they later settled on calling it the Hookless #2 fastener. (Hookless #1 just never made it into production.)

The modern zipper was born and the story is over. (You know that it can't be over—there are more words below!)

But wait! The company had one big problem. It may have solved the fastener's problems, but no one wanted it. For years the company tried to market the newfangled device, but it failed to catch on. Too many people remembered the problems of the old C-Curity and Plako fasteners and had no interest in getting involved with the product again. Others balked at the high price of the contraption. In an effort to avoid the past, the company officially changed its name to the Hookless Fastener Company.

The first steady use of the zipper was actually during World War I. A New York City tailor named Robert J. Ewig designed a zippered aviator's waistcoat that just happened to have the trademarked name of *Zip*. Surprisingly, that's not where the term zipper comes from. Ewig's vests were a failure, so he then designed a zippered money belt, which proved to be very popular with sailors because their uniforms lacked pockets. Approximately 24,000 of these belts were sold, but demand quickly died off once the war was over.

In 1919, the *Locktite* tobacco pouch proved to be the first successful zippered product. By the mid-1920s, nearly two hundred thousand pieces were produced each year. The fastener was slowly making its way into a wide variety of products, but it was still basically considered a novelty item. More than thirty years after the zipper's invention, widespread acceptance still seemed far out of reach.

This would all change in 1921. A B. F. Goodrich engineer by the name of Frederick H. Martin had a brainstorm and placed the fastener on a pair of rubber galoshes, originally called the Mystic Boot. The president of the company decided to change the name to the Zipper (Sound familiar?). Oddly, the term Zipper was a B. F. Goodrich trademark for the boot, not the fastener. The product was a smash hit and Hookless had a tough time trying to keep up with demand for the fasteners. By the late 1920s, demand for the boots died out, but the name stuck.

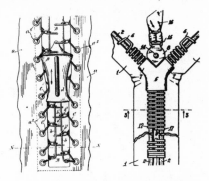

Production of the zipper soared from approximately 110,000 in 1920 to more than 17 million in 1929. The rest of the world seemed stuck in the dark Compare the patent images of Whitcomb Judson's Shoe Fastening device on the left with Gideon Sundback's Separable Fastener on the right. It took many years and lots of trial and error to move from the original zipper to what we have today.

recesses of the Great Depression, but Hookless Fastener just continued to grow.

Of course, any good product attracts imitations and the zipper was certainly no exception. Hookless was constantly fighting it out in patent court. Unfortunately, the zipper may have been hard to perfect, but once it was, it was very easy to duplicate. In an effort to make its product stand out in the crowd, Hookless adopted the brand name Talon in 1928.

It has long been rumored that real acceptance of the zipper did not occur until the trend setting Edward, the Prince of Wales and soon-to-be king of England, adopted zippered clothing. When he abdicated the throne in 1936, he caused a worldwide sensation. This just happened to coincide with the zipper's explosive popularity. In reality, the zipper's success was due to many years of advertising and the constant pushing of the product.

Talon's exponential growth continued until World War II when the supply of copper, zinc, and nickel that was used to make zippers was cut off. Once the war was over, Talon's zipper patents had expired and the company was faced with competition from all over the world. As the years passed, Talon's share of the market declined.

Which leads to the most frequently asked question about zippers. "What does the YKK on my zipper stand for?" To find out, we must go back to 1934 when a Japanese man named Tadao Yashida started manufacturing zippers. His business was destroyed during an air raid on Tokyo in 1945, yet he was able to rise up from the ashes and recover. In 1948, he dubbed his zippers YKK, which stands for Yoshida Kogyo Kabushiki Kaisha. (No wonder they shortened it to YKK—try to fit that long name on a tiny zipper pull tab.) This roughly translates into English as Yoshida Company Limited. Today, YKK is the largest zipper manufacturer in the world, surpassing the output of Talon years ago.

Not only has the zipper become a basic part of our wardrobes but it has also become a part of our vocabulary. For example, when my students are talking out of turn, I tell them to "Put a zipper on it." So now that we have zipped through the history of the zipper, we can now consider this matter all zipped up.

Useless? Useful? I'll leave that for you to decide.

nikola tesla

he makes thomas edison look like a dummy

Here's a task for you to try:

Go check your encyclopedia to find the answers to the following questions (answers are given in parentheses):

1) Who invented the radio? (Marconi)

2) Who invented the x-ray machine? (Roentgen)

3) Who invented the vacuum tube amplifier? (De Forest)

In fact, while you're at it, check to see who discovered the fluorescent bulb, neon lights, the speedometer, the automobile ignition system, and the basics behind radar, the electron microscope, and the microwave oven.

Chances are that you will see little mention of a guy named Nikola Tesla, one of the most famous scientists in the world at the turn of the century. In fact, few people today have ever heard of the guy. In many ways we can thank Thomas Edison and his crew at General Electric for taking care of that.

Tesla was considered, and still is by many, to be an eccentric who talked of death rays that could destroy ten thousand airplanes at a distance of 250 miles. He claimed to be able to split the Earth in two. In the late 1800s, Tesla believed that both voice and image could be transmitted through the air, and essentially told Edison to take his DC electrical system and stick it you know where. He had a peculiar distaste for pearls and forbade any of his female employees from wearing them. Even more strangely, he would calculate the volume of all his food before he ate it.

In other words, anyone that has even heard of Tesla probably considers him to be a first-class wacko.

But the times are a-changin'.

Excluding his peculiarities, which he picked up in the latter part of his life, Tesla invented every single one of the items mentioned at the beginning of this story (but gets no credit) and much, much more. Look around you and chances are Tesla is somehow responsible for most of the things that make modern life so modern.

No doubt about it, Nikola Tesla was the greatest mind since da Vinci.

So who was this genius?

Little Nicky Tesla was of Serbian heritage and was born in Smiljan, Croatia (then Astro-Hungarian empire), way back in 1856. He had an extraordinary memory and learned to speak six languages. Tesla spent four years at the Austrian Polytechnic Institute in Gratz studying math, physics, and mechanics.

What made Tesla great, however, was his amazing understanding of electricity. Remember that this was a time when electricity was still in its infancy.

When Tesla first came to the United States in 1884, he went to work for Thomas Edison. Edison had all sorts of problems with his DC system of electricity. He promised Tesla big bucks in bonuses if he could get the bugs out of the system. Tesla ended up saving Edison over $100,000 (millions of $$$ by today's standards), but Edison refused to live up to his end of the bargain. Tesla quit and the Edison people put considerable effort into trying to squash Tesla's genius. That is one of the main reasons that Tesla is unknown today.

Tesla devised a better system for electrical transmission—the AC (alternating current) system that we use in our homes today.

AC offered great advantages over the DC system. By using Tesla's newly improved transformers (he didn't invent them), AC voltages could be stepped up and transmitted over long distances through thin wires. DC could not because it required a large power plant every square mile while transmitting through very thick cables.

Of course, a system of transmission would be incomplete without devices to run on them. So, Tesla invented the motors that are used in nearly every appliance in your house. This was no simple achievement; scientists of the late 1800s were convinced that no motor could be devised for an alternating current system, making the use of AC a waste of time. After all, if the current reverses direction sixty times a second, the motor will rock back and forth and never get anywhere. Tesla solved this problem easily and proved everyone wrong.

Word began to spread about his AC system and it eventually reached the ears of George Westinghouse.

Tesla signed a contract with Westinghouse under which he would receive $2.50 for each kilowatt of AC electricity sold. Suddenly, Tesla had the cash to start conducting all the experiments he ever dreamed of.

He began using fluorescent bulbs in his lab some forty years before industry "invented" them. At World's Fairs and similar exhibitions, he took glass tubes and molded them into the shapes of famous scientists' names; the first neon signs which we see all around us today. Tesla also designed the world's first hydroelectric plant, located in Niagara Falls. In addition, he patented the first speedometer for cars.

But Edison had too much money invested in his DC system, so General Electric did its best to discredit Tesla at every turn. Edison constantly tried to show that AC electricity was far more dangerous than his DC power.

Tesla counteracted by staging his own marketing campaign. At the 1893 World Exposition in Chicago (attended by 21 million people), he demonstrated how safe AC electricity was by passing high-frequency AC power through his body to power light bulbs. He then was able to shoot large lightning bolts from his Tesla coils to the crowd without harm. Nice trick!

When the royalties owed to Tesla started to exceed $1 million, Westinghouse ran into financial trouble. Tesla realized that if his contract remained in effect, Westinghouse would be out of business and he had no desire to deal with the creditors. His dream was to have cheap AC electricity available to all people. Tesla took his contract and ripped it up! Instead of becoming the world's first billionaire, he was paid $216,600 outright for his patents.

In 1898, he demonstrated to the world the first remote-controlled model boat at Madison Square Garden. He had every intention of selling his invention for use as a remote-controlled, unmanned torpedo, but the War Department declined. So you can thank Tesla for the invention of those remote-controlled planes, cars, and boats, and televisions.

Tesla's biggest dream was to provide free energy to the world. In 1900, backed by $150,000 from financier J. P. Morgan, Tesla began construction of his so-called "Wireless Broadcasting System" tower on Long Island, New York. This broadcasting tower was intended to link the world's telephone and telegraph services, as well as transmit pictures, stock reports, and weather information worldwide. Unfortunately, Morgan cut funding when he realized that it meant *free* energy for the world.

Many stories claim that the U.S. government destroyed the tower during World War 1 for fear that the German U-boat spies would use the tower as a landmark to navigate by. In reality, Tesla ran into financial trouble after Morgan cut funding for the project, and the tower was sold for scrap to pay off creditors.

The world thought he was nuts. After all, transmission of voice, picture, and electricity was unheard of at this time.

What the world didn't know, however, was that Tesla had

already demonstrated the principles behind radio nearly ten years before Marconi's supposed invention. In fact, in 1943 (the year Tesla died), the Supreme Court ruled that Marconi's patents were invalid because of Tesla's previous descriptions. Still, most references do not credit Tesla with the invention of radio. (Side note: Marconi's radio did not transmit voices—it transmitted a signal—something Tesla had demonstrated years before.)

Toward the end of his life, the press started to exaggerate Tesla's claims.

Tesla reported that he had received radio signals from Mars and Venus. Today we know that he was actually receiving the signals from distant stars, but too little was known about the universe at that time. Instead, the press had a field day with his "outrageous" claims.

In his Manhattan lab, Tesla made the earth into an electric tuning fork. He managed to get a steam-driven oscillator to vibrate at the same frequency as the ground beneath him (like Ella Fitzgerald breaking the glass with her voice in those old Memorex commercials).

The result? An earthquake on all the surrounding city blocks. The buildings trembled, the windows broke, and the plaster fell off the walls.

Tesla contended that, in theory, the same principle could be used to destroy the Empire State Building or even possibly split the Earth in two. Tesla had accurately determined the resonant frequencies of the Earth almost sixty years before science could confirm his results.

Don't think he didn't attempt something like splitting the Earth open. (Well, sort of.)

In his Colorado Springs lab in 1899, he sent waves of energy all the way through the Earth, causing them to bounce back to the source. (This same basic principle provides the foundation for today's accurate earthquake seismic stations.) When the waves came back, he added more electricity to it.

The result? The largest man-made lightning bolt ever recorded—130 feet!—a world's record still unbroken! The accompanying thunder was heard twenty-two miles away. The entire meadow surrounding his lab had a strange blue glow, similar to that of St. Elmo's Fire. Unfortunately, he blew out the local power plant's equipment, and he was never able to repeat the experiment.

At the beginning of World War I, the government desperately searched for a way to detect German submarines. The government put Thomas Edison in charge of the search for a good method. Tesla proposed the use of energy waves—what we know today as radar—to detect these ships. Edison rejected Tesla's idea as ludicrous, and the world had to wait another twenty-five years until it was invented.

His reward for a lifetime of creativity? The prized (to everyone but Tesla) Edison Medal! A real slap in the face after all of the verbal abuses Tesla took from Edison.

The stories go on and on.

Industry's attempt (obviously very successful) to purge him from the scientific literature had driven him into exile for nearly twenty years. Lacking capital, he was forced to place his untested theories in countless notebooks.

The man who invented the modern world died nearly penniless at age eighty-six on January 7, 1943. More than two thousand people attended his funeral.

In his lifetime, Tesla received over one hundred different patents. He probably would have exceeded Edison's record number if he wasn't always broke. He could afford very few patent applications during the last thirty years of his life.

Unlike Edison and many other inventors of his time, Tesla was an original thinker whose ideas typically had no precedent in science. Unfortunately, the world does not financially reward people of Tesla's originality. It only awards those who take these concepts and turn them into a refined, useful product.

Scientists today continue to scour through his notes. Our top scientists are just now proving many of his far-flung theories. For example, the bladeless disk turbine engine that he designed, when coupled with modern materials, is proving to be among the most efficient motors ever designed. His patented experiments with cryogenic liquids and electricity provided the foundation for modern superconductors. He talked about experiments that suggested particles with fractional charges of an electron—something that scientists in 1977 finally discovered—quarks!

Wow!

Maybe history will at last recognize a true genius when it sees one.

Useless? Useful? I'll leave that for you to decide.

PART 4:

hmmm

george washington

he was really the ninth president of the united states!

Quick—Who was the first president of the United States? I'm sure that George Washington was your best guess. After all, no one else comes to mind. But think back to your history books. The United States declared its independence in 1776, yet Washington did not take office until April 30, 1789.

So who was running the country during these initial years of this young country? It was the first eight U.S. presidents. In fact, the first president of the United States was one John Hanson.

I can hear you now, *John who?*

John Hanson, the first president of the United States. Don't go checking the encyclopedia for this guy's name. Only if you're extremely lucky will you find even a brief mention of him. Little has ever been written about the life of this man. Hanson is one of those great men whose name has been lost to history.

The new country was actually formed on March 1, 1781, with the adoption of the Articles of Confederation. Although this document was actually proposed on June 11, 1776, it was not agreed upon by Congress until November 15, 1777. Maryland refused to sign it until Virginia and New York ceded their western lands. (Maryland was afraid that these states would gain too much power in the new government from such large amounts of land.)

Although he was the first president of the United States, President John Hanson is largely forgotten today.

Once the signing took place in 1781, a president was needed to run the country.

John Hanson was chosen unanimously by Congress, which included George Washington. In fact, all the other potential candidates refused to run against him, as he was a major player in the revolution and an extremely influential member of Congress. In a letter to Hanson, George Washington wrote, "I congratulate your excellency on your appointment to fill the most important seat in the United States."

As the first president, Hanson had quite the shoes to fill. No one had ever been president and the role was poorly defined. His actions in office would set precedent for all future presidents.

He took office just as the Revolutionary War ended. Almost immediately, the troops demanded to be paid. As would be expected after any long war, there were no funds to meet the salaries. All the members of Congress ran for their lives, leaving Hanson as the only guy left running the government. He somehow managed to calm the troops down and hold the country together. If he had failed, the government would have fallen almost immediately and everyone would have been bowing to a king or queen.

Hanson, as president, ordered all foreign troops off American soil, as well as the removal of all foreign flags. This was quite a feat, considering the fact that so many European countries had had a stake in the United States since the days following Columbus.

Hanson established the Great Seal of the United States, which all presidents have since been required to use on all official documents.

President Hanson also established the first Treasury Department, the first Foreign Affairs Department, and named the first secretary of war.

Lastly, he declared that the "twenty-eighth day of November next, as a solemn Thanksgiving to God." Does this thing called Thanksgiving ring a bell?

The Articles of Confederation only allowed a president to serve a one-year term during any three-year period, so Hanson actually accomplished quite a bit in such little time.

Seven other presidents were elected after him—Elias Boudinot (1782-83), Thomas Mifflin (1783-84), Richard Henry Lee (1784-85), John Hancock (1785-86), Nathan Gorman (1786-87), Arthur St. Clair (1787-88), and Cyrus Griffin (1788-89)—all prior to Washington's taking office.

So what happened?

Why don't we ever hear about the first eight presidents of the United States?

It's quite simple—the Articles of Confederation didn't work well. The individual states had too much power and nothing could be agreed upon. A new doctrine needed to be written; something we know as the Constitution.

And that leads us to the latest controversy.

I have received numerous complaints over the years stating that I have the wrong image associated with this story. My picture is of a white man and many people tell me that the real John Hanson was actually a black man. I have been accused many times of being part of a conspiracy to hide the fact that the first President of the United States was of African heritage.

The outcome of this debate is actually quite simple. There were two men named John Hanson.

The man who served as president was born in Mulberry Grove, Maryland, on April 13, 1721, and died on November 15, 1783.

Little is known about the second John Hanson except that he was a "senator from Bassa County" and that he was somehow involved in the United States' efforts to resettle African-Americans in Liberia. His daguerreotype, located on the Library of Congress Web site and dated "between 1856 and 1860," is definitely of a black man.

Just do a bit of math to prove that the Library of Congress image could not be that of the first president. The man who served as our first president died fifty-six years before photography was introduced to the world in 1839, so no photographic images of him would exist. Personally, I would have loved for the first president of the United States to have been a black man. This would have made for a great story, but it would have been an untrue one.

Useless? Useful? I'll leave that for you to decide.

emperor norton I

the u.s.a.'s first and only emperor

Yes, you read the above title correctly. At one time the United States of America did have an emperor. During his reign, he was known as the one and only Emperor Norton I. As perplexing as this may seem in a country where the people elect its political leaders, this story is totally true. Just read on to find out more.

Unlike most kings, queens, princes, and princesses, Emperor Norton was not born into royalty. In fact, he was just another nobody like the rest of us. Although no exact birth record can be found, Joshua Abraham Norton was born to Jewish parents in London around 1818. When Norton was two years old, his parents picked up and moved the entire family to the Cape of Good Hope in South Africa.

Norton somehow managed to wind up in San Francisco in 1849. This was Gold Rush time in California and he was there to stake his claim by selling supplies to the miners. By 1853, he was worth an estimated quarter of a million dollars through his various mercantile and land deals. He was a wealthy man, even by today's standards.

During this period of time, China was experiencing a terrible famine and placed a ban on the export of rice. The price of rice in San Francisco climbed from four cents to thirty-six cents per pound. Norton then heard the words that would change his life forever: a ship with two hundred thousand pounds of rice was arriving from Peru. He knew exactly what to do; he would purchase all of the rice and control the market. Surely the price of rice would skyrocket and Norton would reap all of the profits.

Well, Norton gambled his fortune on December 22, 1852, and lost. Shipload after shipload of Peruvian rice showed up in port over the next few weeks and the price of rice plummeted. Norton was in debt and was forced to declare bankruptcy in 1858. Yes, Joshua A. Norton was now penniless.

In the months following his bankruptcy, Norton seemed to disappear off the face of the Earth. But, this would all change on September 17, 1859. The United States was about to crown its first emperor.

Joshua A. Norton appeared at the offices of the San Francisco *Evening Bulletin* with the following proclamation:

> *At the peremptory request of a large majority of the citizens of these United States, I, Joshua Norton, formerly of Algoa Bay, Cape of Good Hope, and now for the past nine years and ten months of San Francisco, California, declare and proclaim myself Emperor of these U.S., and in virtue of the authority thereby in me vested, do hereby order and direct the representatives of the different States of the Union to assemble in the Musical Hall of this city on the 1st day of February next, then and there to make such alterations in the existing laws of the Union as may ameliorate the evils under which the country is laboring, and thereby cause confidence to exist, both at home and abroad, in our stability and integrity.*
> *—Norton I,*
> *Emperor of the United States*

The editor of the paper, Deacon Fitch, was amused by Norton's claim and decided to run the story in the paper.

People began to take notice almost immediately. No one really believed that he was the emperor of the United States, but they saw no harm in playing along.

His uniform consisted of an old donated army coat and boots. Add to that a plumed hat, a donated sword, and assorted imperial epaulets, and you have one very royal emperor.

The Emp (as those close to him, meaning myself, called him) proudly walked the streets of San Francisco. While on these excursions, he set out to rid the world of its ills. He simply ruled by decree. For example, with the country on the verge of the Civil War, he abolished the Union. If people complained that taxes were too high, he ordered them lowered. (Don't you wish that he was around today?)

Newspapers competed to publish his proclamations. They did this for one very good reason—the proclamations sold more papers. When the papers needed to boost circulation, they simply made up new Norton proclamations.

Businesses also reaped the benefits of the Emp's presence. If a clothier wanted to sell more clothing, he simply placed a sign in the window stating that the store was the Official Clothier of Emperor Norton (whether it actually was or not). If you wanted to see more patrons in your restaurant, you claimed that the emperor ate there. You get the idea. Sounds like the "George Washington Slept Here" scheme that they have on the eastern coast of the United States.

Soon the word spread about the emperor. People visiting the city purchased statues, postcards, and other souvenirs of the Emp. Yes, he became the city's first tourist trap.

Unlike most rulers, Emperor Norton did his best to stay in touch with his people. He attended every public function and meeting (a large upholstered chair was always reserved for him in the state legislature). He never had a chauffeured coach, instead he always walked or rode his bicycle. He patrolled the streets making sure that police officers were doing their jobs. If he saw people performing kind acts, he would ennoble them. His crowning of the common folk with titles was very popular among the children. They would follow him picking up litter and doing kind deeds in the hope of being crowned king or queen for a day. (Some claim that this is where the expression comes from.)

Emperor Norton did not have the fortune that most other rulers possess. His expenses, however, were few. He was allowed to dine for free in any restaurant of his choice. Three seats at the opening of every theatrical performance were reserved for the Emperor and his two dogs, Lazarus and Bummer. The local Masonic Lodge, of which he was once a member, paid for his small apartment. The city apparently picked up the costs of his uniform.

For money, Norton issued his own imperial bonds, which were usually issued in values from fifty cents to two dollars. These notes were actually produced by the printing firm of Cuddy & Hughes. Each note allowed the bearer to collect the face value plus seven percent interest at maturity, which was apparently in the year 1880. Since the notes had no real value at the time, the best one could do would be to convert it to a new note payable in 1900. Today, the bonds are quite rare and are worth a good chunk of money.

Even the best of emperors cannot live forever. Emperor Norton died on January 8, 1880. The *New York Times* reported that he "dropped dead at the corner of California and DuPont streets, in that city." He was on his way to a scientific conference.

Emperor Norton's funeral was attended by a reported thirty thousand people. Police had to be called in to control the crowds. He was buried in the city's Masonic cemetery.

In 1934, his remains had to be moved to Woodlawn cemetery in Colma. Fifty-four years after his death, he still captured the imagination of San Francisco. Flags throughout the city were lowered and businesses actually closed their doors in his honor. Approximately sixty thousand people attended the ceremony, which featured full military honors. His new granite tombstone was engraved *Norton I, Emperor of the United States, Protector of Mexico, Joshua A. Norton, 1819–1880.*

Many have come to question Norton's sanity. Did he really believe that he was emperor? Or did he have everyone fooled into thinking that he was? Sane or not, he offers an example that modern politicians should be forced to study.

Don't assume that royalty ends in the United States with the death of Emperor Norton. My friend Kelly has proclaimed herself to be Princess Kelly. Please refer to her as such and feel free to forward all of your cash and jewels to her.

Useless? Useful? I'll leave that for you to decide.

pennies for college

a college education for just pennies

It is no big secret that a college education is a very expensive investment. Parents and students all face the reality that they will be paying off those darn student loans for many years to come.

But wait! There is a better way.

Just use your brainpower. Focus on the problem (lack of money) and a possible solution (sorry, the chance of being adopted by Bill Gates is not a viable option).

A guy named Mike Hayes focused on his lack-of-capital problem and came up with an incredible scheme to solve it.

Let's zoom back to 1987. Here we find Mike as a freshman chemistry major at the University of Illinois. Like many others, he is pondering over paying for his education—one that he figures will cost him $28,000 over four years.

Then the brainstorm hit him.

Mike wrote to columnist Bob Greene of the *Chicago Tribune* and asked for his help. The help was simple: Bob would ask each of his millions of readers to send just one penny to help finance Mike's college education.

I know it sounds ridiculous.

But then, what is a penny? Look around you and I bet there is a penny being ignored. Is it in the cushions of your sofa? Under the bed? In your coat pocket? Most people won't even expend the energy to bend over and pick up a penny sitting on the sidewalk.

Well, Bob Greene decided to play along with Mike's crazy scheme and published the column on September 6, 1987. Of course, asking for a penny is fine, but getting people to actually send one is another story. After all, we are a society of couch potatoes. I'm sure that many just read the column and gave a chuckle.

And there was another catch. You can't send a penny through the mail for free. Back then it cost 22 cents to mail a first-class envelope. In other words, your penny donation was really going to cost you about a quarter.

Surely a scheme like this could never work. Mike was asking for a tremendous amount of pennies. Think about it—$28,000 translates into 2.8 million pennies. That's a big wad of pocket change to ask for.

Once the newspaper article appeared, the mail came pouring in. They were all addressed to "Many Pennies for Mike" at his home in Rochelle, Illinois. Some letters were the typical letters of complaint. These people complained that Mike had no right to ask for this money. He was an average middle-class white male; surely, many others should get the money before Mike.

But then, no one *forced* anyone to mail Mike his or her donation.

After one month of collecting, Bob Greene followed up on his article. At that point, the Many Pennies for Mike fund had received about seventy thousand donations. The donations ranged from the one penny asked for to several checks for $100. The average of all donations was estimated to be 34 cents per envelope. In other words, Mike had raked in approximately $23,000! He was only $5,000 short of his goal.

Ninety-five percent of the envelopes had a letter enclosed. One person wrote, "I'm seventy-six years old. Here's a penny. If you use it to buy drugs I hope a bolt of lightning strikes you dead." Another letter from Debra Sue Maffett (Miss America 1983) was signed "love" and included a check for twenty-five smackeroos.

In the end, Mike did get his $28,000 and a bachelor's degree in food science. No one really knows how much more money came in, but Mike agreed to set up an educational scholarship fund with the excess.

One can't help but wonder what the IRS thought about this scheme. They probably changed all of their regulations to make sure that the government will get all the money in the future.

Useless? Useful? I'll leave that for you to decide.

fu-go

the strangest weapon of world war II

You may find this very hard to believe, but the first intercontinental bombing mission was actually conceived and successfully targeted at the continental United States. Now take a trip back through your memory banks. Think about everything that you ever learned about World War II. Are you able to place this series of attacks?

Could it be Japanese kamikazes? No, they attacked American ships, never the continent. The Japanese had a similar kamikaze submarine program, called the Kaitan, that actually caused damage to the U.S. coast at the time, but this would never qualify as an intercontinental attack.

Perhaps it was the Germans? No, they never touched us, either.

Actually, what we're talking about here is the Japanese Fu-Go program (just in case you missed the title at the top of the page). The Fu-Go plan was actually one of the most mysterious and unique military bombing assaults ever to occur.

You see, the Japanese quickly realized during WWII that the American continent was just too far out of reach, so it remained unaffected by the ravages of the war. Their solution was to construct paper balloons that would cross the Pacific and bomb the United States.

Now, I must admit that when I first heard about this story I was thrown off a bit. I have always associated Japan and balloons with origami. You know—those little folded paper balloons that you made in elementary school. I just could not conceive how anyone could create a tiny paper balloon and expect it to cross the mighty Pacific and harm the United States.

Boy, was I wrong!

These tiny paper balloons that I had imagined actually measured nearly thirty-three feet in diameter and were filled with hydrogen gas. Each balloon was crafted from tissue paper made from the Kozo bush, which is very similar to the American sumac, and consisted of over six hundred pieces of paper that were glued together with an adhesive known as Konnyaku-nori, manufactured from a type of Japanese potato. The balloons were waterproofed with, get this, fermented green persimmon juice!

The making of these balloons was no small effort. In fact, it took nearly two years of testing and an investment of nearly 9 million yen (approximately 2 million prewar U.S. dollars) to get the program launched. The cost of each balloon was estimated to be slightly less than 10,000 yen (2,300 prewar dollars). Thousands of Japanese citizens participated in the manufacture of these balloons, although everyone was kept in the dark as to what was actually being made. Most of the labor force consisted of children who were released from school early so that they could devote their energies to the war effort.

The balloons were designed to rise to a height between thirty-two thousand and thirty-eight thousand feet and to stay aloft for some sixty-five to seventy hours. At this height, they would be carried by the jet stream (which was unknown to the rest of the world at the time) at a speed of 100 to 200 miles per hour to the United States.

The design was actually quite ingenious. Each balloon carried five or six incendiary bombs and one conventional bomb.

The balloons were equipped with up to thirty six-pound sand-bags for ballast. These sandbags were released one at a time by an aneroid barometer trigger every time the balloon dipped below thirty thousand feet. Once the last sandbag was released, the designers figured that the balloon would be over the United States and an onboard bat-tery lit a series of fuses to release the bombs. Finally, a demolition charge was set off to destroy any evidence of the balloon's existence.

A captured Fu-Go balloon that was inflated for U.S. Navy tests. (National Archives)

Well, in theory that's how it was supposed to work. Reality was another story.

The first balloons were actually released in June 1944 and not a single one actually made it across the Pacific. Each balloon was fitted with a radio transmitter, which allowed the designers to track their paths.

The Japanese were forced to go back to the drawing board. A new version of the balloon was completed in October 1944. The Japanese had actually planned for 15,000 balloons to be built, but in the end, 10,000 were actually constructed and 9,300 launched.

The first of the newly designed balloons was launched on November 3, 1944. Two days later, on November 4, the first signs of debris were spotted floating about sixty miles off the coast of California. (No, my math isn't wrong. Due to the International Date Line, there was a two-day difference in time). This balloon didn't cause concern because it was loaded with radio equipment and assumed to be a weather balloon that had gone astray.

Over the next month, fragments of balloons started to show up in various locations and scientists were able to construct a rudimentary picture of what the weapon looked like. The U.S. government quickly determined that they posed little danger. They simply could not carry enough high explosive to cause any serious damage. The government was actually more concerned that these balloons could carry biological agents such as the plague or anthrax and infect major portions of the continent. Also, there was worry about the response of the American people once they learned about this weapon. The psychological panic could have been greater than any threat the bombs themselves could have ever caused.

In late December 1944, the media reported on the finding of a balloon in Thermopolis, Wyoming. The U.S. government realized that it needed to keep a lid on this story and requested that newspaper editors and radio broadcasters stop reporting on the Japanese balloons. If word leaked out that the bombings had even the slightest amount of success, the Japanese would just send more. Surprisingly, the media cooperated and the Japanese never learned that a single balloon reached the continent until after the war ended (neither did American citizens—these balloons were responsible for an extremely large number of UFO sightings).

Sand samples taken from the ballast of recovered balloons were handed over to the United States Geological Survey for examination. It had been assumed that the balloons were launched at sea, but several months later the USGS reported, based mainly on fossil evidence, that they had narrowed it down to two launch locations in Japan. Intensified bombing raids of Japan destroyed much of the country's ability to produce and launch the balloons. Since the Japanese high command had concluded that the balloons were not reaching the United States, little effort was made to repair the facilities, and the program was shot down in April 1945.

So, how much damage did these bombs cause?

Actually, very little. The Japanese had the impression that the West Coast of the United States consisted of vast forests. They believed that if they could start forest fires, they could instill panic in the American people. But the Japanese made a major blunder; almost all of the balloons were sent during the winter and the rainy season when nothing would burn easily.

Sadly, on May 5, 1945 (after the project was abandoned), six people were killed by one of the Fu-Go bombs. It appears that a preacher and his wife decided to take a group of children on a Sunday picnic on Gearhart Mountain near Bly, Oregon. While Reverend Archie Mitchell was parking the car, one of the children stumbled across a metallic object. When the kids tried to move it, there was an explosion. Elsie Mitchell and five children aged 11 to 13 were killed. These are the only known deaths on the mainland United States from enemy attack during World War II. In 1950, a memorial was erected on the site. A bronze plaque states "Dedicated to those who died here May 5, 1945, by Japanese bomb explosion. The only place on the American continent where death resulted from enemy action during World War II."

To add a strange twist to this story, another balloon managed to momentarily knock out power to the Hanford Engineering Works in eastern Washington state. This just happened to be an atomic energy plant that was producing uranium slugs for the atomic bomb that would later be dropped on Japan. Backup devices kicked in, but production at the plant was set back for three days and caused a slight delay to the Manhattan Project. Just think of the nuclear disaster that would have occurred if the cooling system had totally failed (remember Chernobyl?).

It is estimated that approximately 1,000 Fu-Go balloons made it to the North American continent, while only 285 were actually discovered. The balloons were found as far north as Alaska and as far south as Mexico. While most of the balloon sightings were concentrated near the Pacific Coast, two balloons found their way to Michigan.

Obviously, the Fu-Go program was not a great success. The efforts that the Japanese put into launching the balloon offense were much greater than the damage caused. Yet, if the balloons had been launched during one of those hot, dry California summers, they could have caused major damage. Even worse, the Japanese could have used them to deliver biological or chemical agents (they chose not to because they were afraid that the United States would retaliate in the same fashion).

Maybe we should stop spending billions of dollars to create just one single fighter plane and look into some cheaper alternatives. Just think—we could replace our atomic weapons with billions of gas-filled balloons! They wouldn't have to do very much—just the sheer numbers of them could be a threat.

Useless? Useful? I'll leave that for you to decide.

bat bombs

the other top-secret weapon

You probably know that World War II came to an end shortly after the United States dropped its atomic weapons on the Japanese cities of Hiroshima and Nagasaki. Well, I recently came across an alternative weapon that the United States was working on that had the potential to bring Japan to its knees without the great loss of human life that accompanied the nuclear weapons. What I am talking about here is bats. No, not baseball bats. Living, breathing, mammal bats.

I can't even see you and I can tell that you are a bit puzzled by this . . .

The use of bats to win the war was the brainchild of a Pennsylvania dental surgeon named Lytle S. Adams. You see, Doc Adams was a bit of an inventor in his spare time. His most successful creation had absolutely nothing to do with winning the war. In the 1930s, he came up with a rural air mail system that made it unnecessary for a plane to land to pick up the mail. With his partner Richard du Pont, Adams set up a company named Tri-State Aviation, which was the 1930s answer to Federal Express. Over the years, Tri-State Aviation went through numerous name changes and acquisitions and became a mega-corporation that you may have heard of—US Airways.

On that day that will supposedly live in infamy, December 7,

1941, Adams was driving home from a visit to Carlsbad Caverns in New Mexico when he learned that the Japanese had bombed Pearl Harbor. Almost immediately, those neurons in Doc's brain began firing (misfiring may be a better word). Doc thought about the millions of bats in the Carlsbad caves and concluded that they would be the ticket to win the war.

As crazy as this whole scheme sounds, it all made perfect sense to Doc Adams. Basically, he proposed that small incendiary bombs be attached to a million or more bats, which would then be released from an airplane right before dawn. Prior to flight, the bats would be cooled down and forced into a semi-state of hibernation. Then, when the bomber was over the target, the bats would be dropped. As they fell, the bats would warm up and fly off in all directions. Being creatures of the night, the bats would immediately disperse into all of the nooks and crannies of the highly combustible Japanese buildings. After about fifteen minutes, the time-delayed bombs would ignite hundreds of thousands of fires all around the city. No city in the world could be prepared for such a disaster, so any "bat-bombed" city would be engulfed in flames.

Now, what would you do if you had a crazy scheme like this? Probably not much. But Adams had connections. Adams was also the owner of a then-cutting-edge air mail system and he just happened to take Eleanor Roosevelt, the First Lady of the United States, along on several trips. This placed Doc Adams just one set of ears away from the President. "This man is not a nut," FDR wrote in a memo to his coordinator of information. He continued, "It sounds like a perfectly wild idea but is worth looking into." With FDR's endorsement, if you could call it that, the bat bomb was placed in the hands of the National Defense Research Committee (NDRC) and the Army Air Force.

There were several types of bats that were best suited for carrying bombs, but they were not available in the vast numbers needed to carry out the project. The bat of choice was the

Mexican free-tailed bat, which was common to the caves of New Mexico and Texas. Preliminary tests showed that the most weight that these bats could carry was about ten grams. Further testing eventually proved that they could handle somewhere between fifteen and eighteen grams, which was still not much. This small payload capacity was a big problem in the days before miniaturization. The smallest incendiary bomb that the United States military had weighed in at a little over two pounds! Even a whole pile of bats couldn't get that thing off the ground! There was also great concern over whether the bats could actually survive the extreme conditions that they would experience when the planes lifted them to high altitudes. Clearly, lots of testing would need to be done.

Over the next year, Doc put together a team to work out all of the bugs. They made great progress, yet many of the officials in the military failed to grasp the whole concept and the project was nearly halted many times. Doc was forced to make repeated trips to Washington to keep the "Adams' Plan" going. While on one of these trips, Doc learned that his plan was being confused with another top-secret project that was costing millions of dollars. When Doc returned from his meeting, he made one of the most memorable statements that I have ever heard. "Yeah! We got a sure thing like the bat bomb going, something that could really win the war, and they're j**king off with tiny little atoms. It makes me want to cry."

Since the government was spending so much money on the atomic bomb project, it sent very little Doc Adams' way. He funded a large portion of the project out of his own pocket. (This would later come back to haunt him when the IRS came after him for back taxes, and he had to sell his home to pay off the debt that the government never reimbursed him for.)

Doc made a mock-up of the bat-carrying shell that he proposed for the project. It looked like a conventional aerial bomb, but its interior featured a stack of twenty-six round egg-tray-like compartments designed to hold the bats. In total, each bat bomb could hold 1,040 bats along with the necessary environmental controls and a parachute. The actual sheet-metal casings were manufactured by the Crosby Company, which just happened to be owned by that famous crooner himself, Bing Crosby, and his not-so-famous brother Larry.

The main chemist assigned to the Adams' Plan, Louis Feiser, was in charge of producing a miniature bomb. He chose to use a new incendiary material that he dubbed "Napalm" (It's certainly not unheard of today!) and encapsulated it in a flammable celluloid casing. The total package came in at 17.5 grams.

Initial tests on May 3, 1943, at Muroc Lake in California (now used as a Space Shuttle landing strip) went very poorly

A bat with a bomb attached. It's hard to imagine how such a small animal could fly with such a large payload. (National Archives)

because nearly all of the project components were not complete. A second round of tests followed on May 15, 1943, at a newly constructed field at the Carlsbad Air Force Base in New Mexico. With dummy bombs attached, the bats were dropped from airplanes, the chutes opened, and the bats sought shelter in every nook and cranny that they could find. If the bats were armed with real explosives, the scientists were certain that the buildings would have burned.

Back on the ground, Feiser decided to take advantage of the fact that photographs of the testing were being taken. He took six cooled-down bats and attached the live incendiary to them. He intended for the semihibernating bats to stay put until the bombs went off and blew them to smithereens. (Clearly, animal rights were not of much concern at the time.) He misfigured.

This is where the story gets really good.

The hot desert sun brought the bats back to life and they flew off in all directions. Within minutes, the control tower burst into flames. The barracks erupted into an inferno. The fire then jumped from building to building, setting most of the structures ablaze. The secrecy of the project meant that a crew of firemen could not be on the base while the tests were being performed. When the fire trucks finally did arrive, the guards would not let them out on the airfield. All they could do is watch from the distance as the complex burned to the ground and clouds of black smoke filled the air.

This was certainly a big embarrassment for the members of the Adams' Plan. Yet, it proved that the bat bomb could truly be effective. If six bats could burn down an air force base, just think what a million bats could do to a Japanese city that was largely made from combustible paper materials.

Yet, the Army was not convinced. Support for the Adams' Plan was pulled and the project looked as if it were dead in the water.

Or was it?

It turns out that luck was on the bat team's side, at least for a little while longer. In a strange twist of fate, a Navy general named Louis DeHaven just happened to be watching the disaster that unfolded during the Carlsbad tests. Unlike the Army observers, DeHaven made a very favorable report to his superiors. This recommendation, coupled with a vigorous public relations campaign on Adams' part, convinced the Navy that this was a project that had some potential. In October 1943, the Navy took control and renamed the Adams' Plan. It was now to be known as Project X-Ray. Not only was Doc's name missing from the project, he was missing also. The Navy canned him.

New tests on the bat bomb took place on December 15, 1943, at the Dugway Proving Ground in Utah. Simulated German and Japanese villages were constructed using native construction methods and furnishings. The bat bombs were tested in a series of controlled experiments (with two fire trucks standing by!). The NDRC reported to the Navy that "It is concluded that X-Ray is an effective plan." It was shown that pound-for-pound, a planeload of bats was much more effective at starting fires than any weapon that the United States had in its arsenal at the time.

Based on this success, the Navy ordered that large-scale production start by May 1944. The plan called for the building of up to 1 million bat bombs. Just when it looked as if Adams' crazy dream was about to become a reality, the Navy pulled the plug on the project in March 1945. After some twenty-seven months and approximately $2 million in research, the bats were grounded. To this day, no one can say for sure why the bats never went off to fight the war.

In all the years that have passed since the idea popped into Doc Adams' head, the electronics have been miniaturized and plastic explosives invented. Maybe it is time to take another look at the bat bomb. Who needs atomic weapons when we can get the bats to fight the war for us?

Useless? Useful? I'll leave that for you to decide.

incredible stories of survival

M.

The *Titanic*

the curse of violet jessop

Titanic. Titanic. Titanic.

Everything related to this ship was big. Big ship. Big disaster. Big legacy. Big movie.

I won't bore you with the details of this story. You've probably heard them many times. Besides, we are here to talk about the unsinkable Violet Jessop.

I know what you are thinking. Wasn't that the unsinkable Molly Brown? Yes, but you're thinking about another story. Molly only survived one disaster at sea. Violet Jessop somehow survived three.

First, let's look at Violet's background to see how she wound up in these disasters.

Violet was born on October 2, 1887, in Argentina, just shortly after her parents had emigrated there from Dublin. Her father died when she was eighteen, so her mother made the decision to pull up stakes again and move back to Europe.

By the age of twenty-one Violet had decided upon her life-long career. She was going to become a stewardess. No, not a stewardess on a plane, but on a big ship. Stewardess was just a glorified name for the onboard cabin maids that catered to the rich people's every whining need.

Her first voyage was aboard the Royal Mail's *Orinoco,* which set sail on October 28, 1908. On September 28, 1910, Violet switched to the White Star Line and embarked on the *Majestic.*

At the time, White Star had received an influx in capital from financier J. P. Morgan and embarked on a plan to build the greatest ships of all time. There were to be three of them, the sister ships *Olympic, Titanic,* and *Gigantic.*

For the greatest ships, White Star needed the greatest staff. Their crew was handpicked from every ship in the company's line. Violet Jessop was one of the few selected. She was young, hardworking, and attractive.

The first ship to be launched was the *Olympic.* At the time, it was the largest and finest ship ever to fly the British flag. And Violet Jessop was on board as a stewardess in first class.

The first few voyages of the *Olympic* were uneventful. The fifth trip to sea was not as lucky. On September 20, 1911, under the command of Captain E. J. Smith (yes—the same captain in charge of the *Titanic* when it went down), the *Olympic* collided with the smaller British cruiser HMS *Hawke.* The *Hawke* forced its way into the *Olympic's* hull, ripping a gash nearly forty feet in length below the waterline. This created a big problem for the ships, but they were both able to limp back to port. Completion of the *Titanic* was put off for nearly a month while the *Olympic* underwent emergency repairs.

So? Big deal, you say. Well, the story gets better. Read on . . .

Being one of White Star's prized employees, Violet was transferred to the newly launched *Titanic.*

I think we all know what will happen on this ship.

Yes, Violet was on the ill-fated *Titanic* when it went down in the North Atlantic on April 15, 1912. She was in her room, drowsy from reading, when the *Titanic* crashed into that dreaded iceberg and began her descent to the bottom of the sea. Being an employee, Violet had no intention of getting into a lifeboat until all the passengers were gone. Another ship's lights (most likely the *Californian,* with its engines and radio off) could be seen several miles away and they all expected to be rescued.

It seems that the officers were having a difficult time getting the immigrant women into the lifeboats due to the language barrier. Violet was standing in the background when an officer requested that she get into a lifeboat to set an example for the other women. Violet got in, was handed a baby to hold, and the others followed. Violet's lifeboat was lowered to the water and launched. Violet would realize the next day while floating around the Atlantic that all those she left behind probably perished.

Violet's lifeboat was also the last to be rescued by the *Carpathia,* which had turned back from a journey to the Mediterranean to help with the rescue. The *Carpathia* returned to New York with the survivors and the remains. Violet chose not to publicly speak to anyone and hopped on the first boat back home to England.

After the *Titanic*'s sinking, the *Olympic* was brought back into port for six months of modification. Structural changes were made and additional lifeboats were added to the ship. Once the ship's retrofit was completed, Violet was once again assigned to the *Olympic* and set sail. She stayed on board until World War 1 broke out. Violet decided to help in the war effort by joining the V.A.D. (Voluntary Aid Detachment) as a junior nurse.

At the same time, work had been under way on the third of these great sister ships (only three were ever built), the *Gigantic.* Since *Gigantic* sounded too similar to *Titanic,* the company decided to change its name to the *Britannic.* Then, on November 13, 1915, the *Britannic* was requisitioned by the British Admiralty and was completed as a hospital ship. The ship took her maiden voyage on December 23, 1915.

On November 21, 1916, the *Britannic* departed from Naples and set sail on her sixth voyage in the Aegean Sea.

And guess what? Violet Jessop was a nurse on board. If you see a tragedy about to happen, you are absolutely correct.

While Violet was down in the dining room getting breakfast for a sick woman, she heard a dull, deafening roar and felt the ship shake. The ship had struck a German-planted mine and had begun to sink.

Everyone to the lifeboats!

Violet went back to her cabin and packed her most prized possessions into her apron pockets. She boarded lifeboat number four.

The captain of the ship cranked the engines in a last-ditch attempt to get the ship into shallower water. What the captain did not realize was that the lifeboats were being lowered at the same time. By starting the engines, a whirlpool was created that sucked the lifeboats into the *Britannic's* enormous propellers. Even the best oarsman could not row against the mighty current.

A few minutes after Violet's lifeboat hit the water, she noticed that everyone had jumped overboard into the sea. She turned and saw the gigantic propellers slicing and dicing anything and anyone that came near it.

Violet had no choice but to jump out herself. Unfortunately, she did not know how to swim. She had also made the mistake of placing her coat under her life vest, which meant that she could not remove it when it became waterlogged.

Down she went. (Violet, that is.)

Her buoyant body slowly rose back up.

Crack!

Violet's head crashed into something hard, most likely the bottom of the lifeboat. Then it happened a second time, and a third.

Would Violet survive? You bet. Remember that we are dealing with the unsinkable Violet Jessop!

Violet's nose just barely rose above the water's oscillating waves. She opened her eyes just as another life jacket was floating by. She grabbed it to stay afloat. Her next sight was that of a head split open with its brains falling out. There were body parts and wreckage floating all around her. Quite the gruesome sight.

In the distance, Violet could see the *Britannic* slowly slide beneath the water's surface. The ship was not even one year old, yet it went down in fifty-five minutes. The ship would not be seen again until Jacques Cousteau discovered it on the sea bottom in 1976.

Shortly after the sinking, one of the *Britannic*'s motorboats came to rescue Violet. The damage? Violet's leg was deeply cut and torn up. She would find out years later while getting a dental x-ray that her skull had been severely fractured, but she had had no clue at the time.

Others were not as lucky. While only twenty-eight people perished, many others suffered serious injuries, losing arms and legs. Luckily, the *Britannic* did not have any wounded in its hospital beds at the time, or the death toll might have compared to that of the *Titanic*.

Violet was probably the only *Britannic* survivor to be rescued with her toothbrush in hand. She had learned from the *Titanic* disaster just four years earlier to go back to her cabin to get the toothbrush if you think your ship is about to go under.

After the war, Violet returned to her life as a cabin stewardess. She retired in 1950, after forty-two years at sea. She passed away in May 1971. After her death, Violet's nieces discovered a manuscript that she had written in 1934. It was finally published in 1997 under the title *Titanic Survivor*. Without this manuscript, her story may never have been completely told.

So there you have it. Not only did Violet Jessop have the privilege of being aboard the greatest ships of her time, but also she had the honor of being the only woman to have survived all three of the ill-fated sister ships.

Violet Jessop was one lucky lady. But then, she was a curse on the other passengers of these ships. I don't think I would have been able to sleep comfortably if I'd known she was on the same ship as I was.

Useless? Useful? I'll leave that for you to decide.

poon lim

how did he manage to survive?

People do all kinds of strange things to make a world record.

The world's largest pizza. The longest fingernails. The person who can pull a train with his teeth. The loudest rock concert. And on and on . . .

Yet, there is one world's record that I am certain that no one wants to break.

It is currently held by a guy named Poon Lim. He managed to spend 133 days floating around the South Atlantic in a life raft all by himself.

First, a bit about Poon. He was born on Hainan Island, which is located off the southern coast of China. At the ripe old age of twenty-five, Poon Lim found himself serving as second steward in the British Merchant Navy aboard the S.S. *Benlomond*. He was one of fifty-five crew members sailing from Cape Town, South Africa, to Dutch Guiana (Surinam) in South America.

So far nothing sounds unusual here, until I mention that this was during the height of World War II. The Atlantic was filled with those dreaded German Nazi U-boats. As fate would have it, on November 23, 1942, one of the U-boats spotted the *Benlomond* off the northern coast of Brazil and fired a torpedo at it.

Boom! Direct hit! (You sank my battleship would be the cry of game players years later.)

The ship was sinking rapidly, so Poon Lim and many others jumped overboard into the water. Poon Lim had a life jacket on and swam away from the sinking vessel. His wet clothing only slowed him down, so he was forced to strip it from his body to gain speed. This was a good move on Poon's part, as the ship's boilers exploded and the ship sank below the surface, never to be seen again.

So here's the situation: Imagine that you are in poor Poon's situation. You are floating around the Atlantic Ocean without a lifeboat, struggling to keep your head above water. It's totally dark, you are butt-naked, and land cannot be seen in any direction.

What would you do?

I guess all that you can do is hope for a miracle.

Poon Lim received his miracle. Well, sort of.

You see, Poon was treading water, hoping to spot a life raft. As each crest of a wave came by, he tried to lift himself out of the water to see out into the distance.

At first, he spotted a life raft with five men in it. The sailors were picked up by a U-boat, but after a few minutes below deck, they were escorted back to their raft. A member of the U-boat crew actually spotted Lim struggling in the water. Instead of offering assistance, the enemy pointed his gun at Lim, pretended to fire, and then left him to die. The U-boat descended and Lim was quite positive that the sub was steered directly into the life raft. In everyday terms, the men were basically mowed down. When he was finally rescued (and this would be a very, very long time), Lim's suspicions would be confirmed because the men were never rescued.

But wait!

Poon Lim is still floating around naked in the Atlantic!

After floating in the water for two hours, he spotted a life raft several hundred feet away. Obviously, he swam toward it and hopped in.

It was an eight-foot square raft that consisted of six water-tight drums surrounded by a wooden timber frame. There were two open slat ledges on either side of a central well that measured approximately six by three feet. Stored away on the raft were a ten-gallon tank of water, some flares, and a flashlight. He also found two pounds of chocolate, five tins of evaporated milk, a sack of barley sugar, a bottle of lime juice, and a container of very hard biscuits. Let's face it, the raft wasn't exactly a luxury liner and only a crazy person could have chosen these food items as necessary for survival. He figured that if he limited himself to a few swallows of water and two biscuits for breakfast and dinner, he should be able to stay alive for at least a month.

At first, Poon Lim had great hope. He came quite close to being rescued several times. Seven days into his ordeal, he frantically tried to get the attention of a ship passing by. He set off his flares to get the crew's attention. They did spot him, but once they realized that he was Chinese, they just left him to die. The ship that was passing by did just that; it passed by. (Why do I hear Barry Manilow singing, "We're two ships that passed in the night" here?)

Then he spotted six or seven patrol planes flying overhead. Having no flares remaining, it was difficult for Lim to get their attention. Yet, somehow he did. One plane circled around and dropped a canister of oil to mark the spot and then took off. That night, a violent storm broke out, and Lim was moved far off course. The planes never returned to find him.

Poon Lim quickly realized that he was going to be out at sea for quite some time. He could have chosen to give up and die, but instead decided to use his skills and limited supplies to stay alive.

The raft was equipped with two large pieces of canvas, one of which he used as a roof to protect him from the sun's intense rays. (Remember, he was naked.) Lim fashioned the canvas roof into a catchall to collect rainwater, which he stored in the ten-gallon tank. He took apart the flashlight and used the spring inside to fashion a fishing hook. Next he used his teeth to pull out some of the nails that held the raft together (Ouch!) and pounded them to make additional hooks. Then he fashioned the tough hemp rope on board into a crude fishing line. He used the barnacles growing on his raft as bait.

If all went well, he had the tools to stay alive. Now all he had to do was catch something.

When he finally caught his first fish, he cut it in half with a tin can that held some of the biscuits. He ate half of the fish and put the other half aside to use as additional bait for his next meal. He continued to catch fish and dried them on a line that he rigged up. He was basically making fish jerky.

On one of his many fishing efforts, things did not go exactly as planned. The fish on his line turned out to be a shark. He didn't exactly have Jaws here, but the shark was several feet long and probably just as scary. He pulled the shark in. Assuming that the shark would put up a struggle, he covered his arms with the canvas. The shark attacked him on the raft, so Poon Lim bashed him over the head with the partially filled water container. He cut open the shark and sucked the blood from its internal organs.

Finally, Poon Lim noticed that seagulls were flying in the air. He knew that he had to be close to land, but as you already know, he would still be floating for many more weeks. When his fish supply seemed to dwindle, Lim was determined to catch one of the birds. He grabbed some seaweed from the water and fashioned it into a nest. He placed some of the dead fish next to the nest assuming that the rotting meat would attract the birds. When an unlucky bird happened to land to eat the fish, Poon Lim grabbed it. The bird cut him up quite a bit, but Lim won the struggle in the end.

Then he spotted land. Was he now safe? Of course not. He was floating along the edge of the Amazon jungle. It was too thick and dense for any man to walk through. There was also the new problem of fending off giant snakes and other animals. Since his best tool was a crude knife fashioned from a tin can, Lim felt that it was in his best interest to keep floating on the raft.

And he floated.

And he floated.

On April 5, 1943 (130 days alone), he spotted a fishing boat on the horizon. He flagged the boat down and they sailed toward him. The fishing boat had three Portuguese sailors who helped Lim aboard. Lim had somehow floated all the way to the mouth of the mighty Amazon River. They offered him water and beans, which we can be sure that he took very gratefully. They didn't take him to port immediately, however. Poor Poon Lim had to wait for them to finish their fishing, so it was three more days before being taken to shore. They ended up taking him to a British colonial town in Brazil called Belem.

He spent four weeks in the hospital recovering from his ordeal. He was actually in great shape. His weight was only down by thirty pounds. He had very little appetite and could only drink milk for the longest time. His legs were fairly weak, but he was able to walk unaided. Of course, he had a nice tan!

The British consul arranged for him to return to Britain via Miami and New York. While in Miami, he told his story of survival through a Chinese translator. The U.S. Navy was so impressed by his survival skills that they made a short documentary reenacting his ordeal. They used it for recruitment, but when Poon Lim decided to enlist in the Navy himself, he was turned down for being flat-footed! (I guess that the Navy bureaucrats felt that he didn't meet the minimum requirements needed to ensure survival at sea.)

While in New York on Friday, July 16, 1943, Poon Lim was told that he had been awarded the British Empire Medal, which was the highest civilian decoration for valor, and that he was invited back to England to receive the decoration directly from King George VI himself.

Of course, the company that he worked for couldn't miss a great photo opportunity like this one. The Ben Shipping Liner Company presented him with the legendary corporate gift—you guessed it—a gold watch.

At the end of the war, Poon Lim decided to emigrate to the United States. Unfortunately, the limit of 105 Chinese immigrants had been exceeded, and he was denied citizenship.

Luckily, he was a famous war hero, albeit a flat-footed one. President Harry Truman signed what is known as "Private Law 178" on July 27, 1949, to "provide for admission to, and the permanent residence in, the United States of Poon Lim." Funny, I always thought that it was the United States of America.

When it was pointed out to Poon Lim that he was the holder of the world's record as a sea survivor on a life raft, he was quoted as saying quietly, "I hope that no one will ever have to break that record."

So do I.

Useless? Useful? I'll leave that for you to decide.

mount pelée

how an election killed the entire electorate

Politicians will do almost anything to win an election, even if it means killing off their entire electorate. Such a case occurred in 1902 in the beautiful town of St. Pierre, Martinique.

If you're like me (failed to pay attention in geography class) and don't know exactly where this island is, I will save you the trouble of checking your atlas. Martinique is located in the Caribbean Sea, about four hundred miles northeast of Venezuela.

By the way, Columbus may never have discovered America, but historians are pretty sure that he discovered this tiny island in 1502. (Two questions: 1) How can you discover an island that people already inhabited? and 2) How could Columbus miss an entire continent yet somehow crash into some dinky little island in the middle of nowhere?)

Back to our story:

An election to choose a representative to France from each of the island's two arrondissements (districts) was slated for May 10, 1902. The outcome of the election stood a great chance of changing the balance of power on the island.

In one corner, there was the ruling Progressive Party, which stood for total white supremacy and had ruled the island for centuries. In the opposing corner, the newly formed Radical Party, which represented Martinique's black and mulatto majority. Just three years earlier, in the 1899 elections, a black man named Amédee Knight had been elected as the island's senator. The Progressive Party was determined to make sure that no other black man would hold political office. It was a heated battle of the rich against the poor, black against white.

But even more heat was coming from the giant on which the island was built—Mount Pelée.

In early April, Mt. Pelée started to rumble. It began to spew out clouds of ash and noxious fumes from its crater. The narrow streets of St. Pierre started to become buried in layers of the fine ash.

The people were worried, but no one was more worried than Governor Mouttet. He had just been appointed to his position seven months earlier by the French government, and it would be a great embarrassment to him if both of the elected representatives to France were members of the Radical Party. The election would be a close call and the governor was doing all that he could to manipulate it. The last thing he needed was for people to panic and leave the island. He knew very well that the only people with enough money to leave were the white minority. If they left, the Progressive Party would lose the election to the Radicals. He had to do something to keep them from leaving.

Mouttet persuaded the island's major newspaper, *Les Colonies,* to downplay the dangers of the volcano and to blame the ever-growing panic and fear of Pelée on the Radical Party. For years, the paper had supported the ruling governor on every issue, and this was no exception. Mouttet convinced the editor, Andreas Hurard, that the paper should dismiss any threat of Pelée's danger. Hurard had no choice but to abide by the governor's request, since Mouttet was in a position to cause a great decrease in advertising revenue.

On May 3, a fissure blew on the volcano and the ash and mud destroyed a mountain village and flowed down the river that passed through St. Pierre. The American consul dispatched a telegram to alert Washington to the danger. Mouttet intercepted the telegram and sent his own message stating that the eruption was subsiding and the danger was gone.

Unfortunately, this was not true. Ash continued to rain down and roofs collapsed all around the city. Hundreds of people who lived in the country closer to the volcano had been killed during various eruptive episodes. Those who survived crowded into St. Pierre and its population swelled to about thirty thousand people. The city residents wanted to leave, but Mouttet just could not afford to let this happen. It had been rumored at the time that the governor had given orders to keep the entire population of St. Pierre from leaving.

Coincidentally, on May 7, the volcano Soufrière on the nearby island of St. Vincent erupted. Nearly two thousand people died from its deadly force. The eruption of Soufrière actually offered some comfort to the residents of St. Pierre; they reasoned that the eruption caused the pressure on their volcano to subside.

That same evening, the governor and his wife visited St. Pierre and stayed at the Hotel de l'Indépendance. He was there to help restore the confidence of his people. When he arrived, he realized just how bad things really were and decided that it was time to evacuate the city. He decided to make his announcement after the High Mass celebration scheduled at the cathedral the very next day. Unfortunately, Mouttet would never get to give the evacuation orders. At seven fifty-nine the next morning, several cracking explosions were heard from Mt. Pelée.

It was the beginning of the end.

A large black cloud blew out of the volcano. Lightning bolts shot from the billowing smoke. Even worse, a searing avalanche of volcanic gases and debris raced down the mountain. This glowing cloud, known technically as a *nuee ardente,* moved down the slopes toward St. Pierre.

With temperatures in excess of 1,300 degrees Fahrenheit (700 degrees Celsius), the avalanche moved at speeds in excess of sixty miles per hour.

The last word the outside world would ever hear from the city was at 8:02 A.M. when the St. Pierre telegraph operator sent the message of *"Allez"* (go) to the Fort-de-France operator. Just one minute later, a wireless operator aboard the ship *Pouyer-Quertier* sent the message: "St. Pierre destroyed by Pelée eruption. Send all assistance."

St. Pierre was in flames in seconds. From the distance, scores of blazing people could be seen fleeing the fireball, heading for the apparent safety of the sea. Their scorched flesh sizzled as they entered the water. A wall of flaming rum, which had poured off the docks and trading ships, spread across the water ultimately killing those who made it this far.

Rescue teams were slow to arrive. The distant ships that did see the eruption thought that it was Soufrière and totally bypassed Martinique. The great maritime powers of Great Britain, Japan, Germany, and the United States had all sent help to St. Vincent. They had no idea how much worse things were in St. Pierre.

Of course, rescue teams would have been of little help. The eruption would eventually prove to be the deadliest of the twentieth century and the third deadliest in the past two thousand years.

It was assumed that all thirty thousand residents, including Governor Mouttet and his wife, were boiled alive. Most of the deceased were found stark naked. Their clothes vaporized right off their bodies. The heat was so intense that both glass and steel were easily melted. The city was totally demolished.

When rescuers arrived to search for survivors, they surprisingly found three. Yvette Montferrier, a housewife, had survived by taking shelter in a ditch about one mile outside of town. She was badly scalded and it is not known if she survived more than a few hours or days.

One man, a twenty-eight-year-old cobbler named Léon Compère-Léandre, was lucky enough to have been on the outskirts of the city near the waterfront. Prior to the explosion, refugees had invaded his house and had refused to leave. Instead of arguing

A man looking over the ruins of St. Pierre after the deadly eruption. (Library of Congress)

with them, he took shelter in the basement of his home. When Compère-Léandre emerged after the eruption, he found his house demolished and all of the refugees killed. Though his legs, arms, and chest were bleeding and raw with burns, he managed to get to "Le Trace" (about 3.5 miles away), which was the main road to Fort-de-France. He was picked up by rescuers, taken to the hospital, and nursed back to health. He lived until 1936.

The ultimate twist in this story, however, had to do with a nineteen-year-old man named Auguste Ciparis, who was found in an underground jail cell. He was badly burned, his cell was filled with rubble, and he had to wait three days before rescue arrived.

Why was he there?

It seems that Ciparis was a black man who had been sentenced to death for the murder of a white Frenchman. He was scheduled to hang on Thursday, May 8—the same day as the eruption! Of course, his captors never came to take him away. In a great twist of fate, thirty thousand people, including those who sentenced Ciparis to death, ended up being the ones killed. The man sentenced to die was the only one in the city who survived.

This is tragic irony at its best.

Ciparis was lucky enough to have his sentence commuted. It was later learned that the governor had planned on granting him a pardon in a last-ditch effort to throw the election his way. Ciparis later went on to earn a living as one of the sideshows in the Barnum & Bailey Circus. His act? He spent his days living in a replica of his cell. Ciparis eventually died in 1929.

Useless? Useful? I'll leave that for you to decide.

PART 6:

unbelievable!

gadsby

an *e*-less novel

Did you know that the letter *E* is the most commonly used letter in our alphabet? Some people claim that it is used nearly four or five times as much as any other letter.

Now try to author a paragraph without it. You will quickly find out that it is a difficult thing to do. In fact, this paragraph lacks this bit of information in all of its words.

I had a tough time just writing the last few sentences without the letter *E*. Now try writing a few pages without this character. While you're at it, try writing an entire book. (Such constraints are known as lipograms.)

This surely sounds like an impossibility. Even if you could avoid the letter *E* in your writing, the product would not be easy to read. Think of all the words that you would need to avoid. You would be forced to skip almost any word in the past tense; it seems as if they all end in *ed*. While you're at it, forget about using any number between six and thirty. (You can't cheat by using the numerical equivalent.)

Good luck in writing your book.

But wait! Stop the presses!

It turns out that one man already achieved this goal way back in 1937. His name was Ernest Vincent Wright, and he just happened to author a 50,110-word novel named *Gadsby* that was entirely *E*-less.

Gadsby was not Wright's first effort at writing. This American author had previously completed *The Wonderful Fairies of the Sun* (1896), *The Fairies That Run the World and How They Do It* (1903), and *Thoughts and Reveries of an American Bluejacket* (1918).

Here's a reprint of the first sentence in *Gadsby:*

If Youth, throughout all history, had had a champion to stand up for it; to show a doubting world that a child can think; and, possibly, do it practically; you would constantly run across folks today who claim that "a child don't know anything." (page 10)

And here's another passage:

"Why, good gracious!" said Frank Morgan, "if anybody should sit in that Mayor's chair in City Hall, it's you! Just look at what you did to boost Branton Hills! Until you got it a-going it had but two thousand inhabitants; now it has sixty thousand!" (page 45)

And another:

"Gadsby was walking back from a visit down in Branton Hills' manufacturing district on a Saturday night. A busy day's traffic had had its noisy run; and with not many folks in sight, His Honor got along without having to stop to grasp a hand, or talk; for a Mayor out of City Hall is a shining mark for any politician. And so, coming to Broadway, a booming brass drum and sounds of singing told of a small Salvation Army unit carrying on amidst Broadway's night shopping crowds. Gadsby, walking toward that group, saw a young girl, back toward him, just finishing a long soulful oration, saying— ". . . and I can say this to you, for I know what I am talking about; for I was brought up in a pool of liquor!!" (page 201)

Not everyone can claim that he or she was brought up in a pool of liquor . . .

As you can tell, these passages are quite constrained, although the book is surprisingly fairly easy to read. (Could Wright have used any more semicolons?)

So what would possess a person to want to take on such a task? Wright claims that he had read a four-stanza poem that was entirely e-less along with a statement that this particular letter occurred five times more often than any other letter.

To accomplish this entirely e-less goal, Wright actually tied down the "E" key on his keyboard which, in effect, made the key virtually useless. Somehow, he managed to finish this novel in just 165 days. It clocks in at 267 pages, although the first nine pages are used by Wright to describe his madness for writing this book. Since the book's introduction, as well as the cover, are not actually part of the story, he is able to use the letter E very freely here. The final line of the book is, very understandably: "Note: Not a word containing the letter 'E' has appeared in this story of over 50,000 words."

That's Ernest Vincent Wright reading the manuscript of his E-less book *Gadsby*. Wright only allowed himself to use the letter E in the Introduction to the book, which starts on the page shown above.

This is an incredible feat. But, we have to ask ourselves just one question: Why would anyone even attempt such a useless project?

Apparently this project was even too much for Wright. He died at sixty-six years of age the very day that *Gadsby* was published.

Useless? Useful? I'll leave that for you to decide.

niagara falls-part 1

the day the falls actually went dry

If you have never been to Niagara Falls, then you are missing quite a wondrous sight. It is almost impossible to describe in words the force, fury, and unparalleled beauty of the falls. Prior to diversion of some of its water to the great hydroelectric plants located on the Niagara River, it was estimated that approximately 93 million gallons of water dropped some 190 feet over its edge every minute. Not exactly your typical home shower.

If you happen to be one of those people planning a trip to Niagara Falls for your honeymoon, vacation, or whatever, you'd better hope that the falls actually has water going over it. After all, a dry falls is nothing more than a big rock cliff and we all know that there is nothing special about that.

Perhaps you have heard about the time that the United States Army Corps of Engineers shut off the American Falls by placing a dam across part of the river way back in 1969. However, this did not shut the falls off totally; the water was actually diverted to Horseshoe Falls and the power plants.

What I'm talking about here is the strange series of events that took place on March 29, 1848—the day the falls went totally dry— and there wasn't even a drought.

So what happened? Here's the scoop:

It seems that on the evening of the twenty-eighth, residents accustomed to the falls' roar were awakened by a very strange silence. The mighty Niagara was silent. I suppose that it was like living under the elevated trains in New York City; after a while you don't even notice the noise. But when it's not there you experience an unexplained strange feeling. (At least that's my mom's claim. Every time that I slept over at my grandparents' apartment as a kid, the train would keep me awake all night.)

It's hard to believe that the mighty Niagara could actually stop flowing. (Library of Congress)

Hundreds of people came out of their homes to see what had happened. The residents quickly realized that the falls had diminished to just a few small streams of water. They were positive that the water had been flowing at normal levels when they went to sleep.

No one was quite sure what happened. After all, they couldn't get into an airplane to see what happened upstream. There were no phones to call others. And, of course, they didn't have the luxury of television and radio.

In other words, people were clueless as to what happened.

Some assumed that this was the end of the Earth, the day that many religions had warned about. They filled the churches in the area and prayed for everything to turn out fine.

Others decided to earn some money. Since this was the first time that the riverbed had actually been exposed, souvenir hunters decided to do some hunting. They examined the river floor and found lots of junk—mainly old guns, swords, tomahawks, and rusted artifacts left over from the War of 1812. One enterprising man hauled logs out of the riverbed; after all, it was easier than actually chopping the trees down (no chain saws in these times). Rocks that had always hindered the navigation of boats were blown to smithereens.

So what caused this to happen?

This article from the April 5, 1848, issue of the *Buffalo Daily Courier* describes the day that Niagara Falls went dry.

To this day, no one is exactly sure. The explanation most often cited claims that the wind had been blowing very strongly that day, causing the water level in the river to drop. At the same time, an ice block occurred at the entrance to the Niagara River at the point where it drains from Lake Erie. The result was the dry falls that everyone woke up to. The ice jam lasted for thirty hours and by April 1 the falls had returned to normal. (I guess it was nature's way of playing an April Fools' joke on the residents of Niagara Falls.)

Useless? Useful? I'll leave that for you to decide.

niagara falls—part 2

an unusual contest

While researching the previous story on Niagara Falls, I discovered that the first bridge to ever cross the gorge was being built during this time period. A company headed by Charles Ellet Jr. had contracted to build a suspension bridge to carry carriages, trains, and bipedal humans. (That is, walkers.)

Ellet had one really *big* problem that was keeping him from building the bridge. Since he was proposing a suspension bridge, someone had to figure out a way to get the first cable across the eight-hundred-foot gorge. This was not an easy task. No boat at the time was strong enough to cross the torrential Whirlpool Rapids. Ellet proposed that a rocket be shot across the gorge with a rope attached to it. (Did they even have rockets back then?) Others suggested that a cannon launch a bombshell.

Hmmm. This was a perplexing problem for them.

But as I always tell my students, the best answer is usually the simplest one. Ellet offered a cash prize to the first boy who could fly a kite across the gorge. In no time, kites with very long strings could be seen filling the area sky. No one had any success, however, until a fifteen-year-old boy named Homan Walsh showed up on the scene.

Walsh took a ferry from the American to the Canadian side of the river and then walked two miles to the point above where the bridge was to be built. His first attempt did get his kite, *The Union,* across the gorge, but the string broke on the jagged rocks. He was determined to try again, but his attempt to rescue his kite from the other side was delayed when ice jams put a halt to ferry service for eight days. Walsh succeeded on his second try and took home the cash prize.

With Walsh's string successfully across the gorge, the bridge builders were able to attach a heavier line to the kite string and pull it across. They repeated this procedure back and forth, increasing the line's diameter with each pass until the necessary cable was in place. A service bridge was finished in July 1848. It proved to be so popular that it forced the famous *Maid of the Mist* to transform its role from a ferry service to a sightseeing venture. However, politics then entered the picture and Ellet's firm never completed the project. Just seven years later, John Roebling would build the first bridge capable of carrying the weight of railway traffic across the gorge.

Useless? Useful? I'll leave that for you to decide.

the al-kuwait

how donald duck helped save the day

As you are probably well aware, the ocean bottom is filled with the wrecks of ships that never made it to where they had intended. Some of these ships contained gold and precious jewels. Others went down in battle. Yet the ship that I am about to discuss would have never been even a footnote in history if it were not for the genius of that fictitious cartoon character Donald Duck.

So, let's zoom back to December 1964 where we will find the freighter *Al-Kuwait* sitting on the floor of the Persian Gulf at an eighty-seven-degree list to port.

Big deal, you say.

Well, it was a really big deal to the residents of Kuwait. You see, the ship went down with approximately six thousand sheep on board right in the middle of Kuwait's main source of water. The desalinization plants used to make the seawater drinkable were designed specifically to remove salt. They were not designed to remove the effects of thousands of rotting carcasses. It was obvious that they had to raise the ship to save the water supply, but no one was quite sure how to do it.

The solution actually came from Danish engineer Karl Kroyer, who was working in Kuwait at the time. He remembered reading a May 1949 Walt Disney comic in which Donald Duck was faced with a similar problem—how to raise his uncle Scrooge's sunken yacht. Donald and his three nephews (Huey, Dewey, and Louie, just in case you forgot) came up with a great solution: they filled the yacht up with Ping-Pong balls and floated it to the surface.

Kroyer decided to try a similar approach. Clearly, getting your hands on enough Ping-Pong balls to raise a two thousand-gross-ton cargo ship has never been an easy task. Instead, Kroyer developed a system in which powdered polystyrene was boiled to form pearl-sized air-filled balls. Essentially, he was making his own small Ping-Pong balls right there on the site. Once the bubbles were formed, he intended to pump them down into the ship's hull.

Kroyer arranged for all of the boilers, pumps, and chemicals to be flown from Denmark to Kuwait. We can be quite sure that the machines pumped and pumped and pumped.

So, did this crazy scheme work?

You bet. It took 150 tons of foam, which translates into roughly 27 million polystyrene balls, and three months, but the *Al-Kuwait* was successfully brought back to the surface and towed safely away. The Kuwaiti water supply was saved. The total cost to save the ship was $435,000. Since the ship was insured for $2 million, the insurance company made out very well. What a bargain!

Stories and images of this unusual salvage appeared in print all around the world. This sounded like great publicity, but when BASF, the company that had the contract to raise the ship, applied for a patent on the new process, it was denied. It seems that Donald Duck had beaten the mighty conglomerate to the punch. Since Donald's ingenious solution was already in print, it was considered public knowledge. If the company had never bragged to the world where it had gotten the original idea from, they probably would have received the patent.

And the Kuwaiti people can thank a fictional character named Donald Duck (and his cartoonist, Carl Barks) for saving their water supply.

Useless? Useful? I'll leave that for you to decide.

the baby derby

how many babies can a woman have in ten years?

Let's hop in our time machine and set the clock back to 4:30 P.M. on October 31, 1926. On this date a wealthy Canadian lawyer named Charles Vance Millar died at age seventy-three. He was seated at his desk and just as he was about to speak, his "head fell forward and without a sound he passed away."

Big deal, you say. People die every single day.

That is true. In fact there was nothing unusual about his death at all. His last will and testament is the thing that we are interested in.

Millar never married and did not have any children. A lack of family meant no one to leave his fortune to. Instead, Millar went to extra efforts to make his will a series of practical jokes, all designed to see how far a human being would go for his money.

One clause in his will bequeathed lucrative shares in the Ontario Jockey Club to a judge and a preacher, both of whom were fiery foes of gambling. What did they do? They accepted his gift, going against all that they preached. A third share was left to a man who owned two competing tracks and whose shady nature would have normally barred him from membership.

In another clause, Millar left one share of stock in the Kenilworth Jockey Club racetrack to every Christian minister in town who had expounded "the scripture to the sinners." After much public debate, only a handful of clergy chose to accept the gift. They would later find out that each share was only worth one-half of 1 cent.

He also bequeathed one share of the O'Keefe Brewing Company to every Protestant minister in Toronto. It just so happened that the brewery was under Catholic ownership. This was a time when there was great hostility between the two groups, yet 91 of the 260 eligible clergy accepted the shares valued at $56 each.

The famous part of his will, however, had to do with the so-called Baby Derby.

How did the Baby Derby work?

It was actually quite simple. Millar bequeathed the remainder of his fortune "at the expiration of ten years from my death to give it and its accumulations to the Mother who has since my death given birth in Toronto to the greatest number of children as shown by the Registrations under the Vital Statistics Act." In plain English this means that he left his fortune (estimated to be $100,000) to the woman who produced the most kids during the ten-year period following his death.

Of course, there were many who contested this clause, including his nephews and nieces. Others questioned whether his will contributed to public immorality. Then there was the question of illegitimate and stillborn children. But remember that Millar was a lawyer, so the document was well written. After twelve years of legal wrangling, the case ended up in the Canadian Supreme Court, which upheld the contents of his will.

At first, the contest was thought of as little more than a curiosity. Then, the Great Depression set in and people were desperate for jobs and money. Around the same time, people became aware of the fact that Millar had purchased one hundred thousand shares in a tunnel project. The shares were basically worthless at the time of his death, valued at just $2.00 in total, but the tunnel between Windsor, Ontario, and Detroit, Michigan, actually became a reality. The value of Millar's estate ballooned to approximately $750,000. All of a sudden, Millar's fortune seemed to look very attractive.

Thus began the great derby.

They're off!

Toronto's maternity wards were filled to the brink. The newspapers ran box scores showing which women were in the lead. Of course, special highlight was given to mothers lucky enough to have twins or triplets. The city's department responsible for registering infants became overwhelmed with applications for "forgotten infants" and had to refuse additional requests.

We can be sure that the bookies were taking bets on this one.

Ten years to the minute after Millar's death, the contest was over. After resolving all of the legal questions regarding the will, it was time for the judge to award the prize.

One woman, Pauline Clarke, would have won by today's standards with ten children in ten years, but she was disqualified. Why? Because not all of her children had the same father. It seems that she had children with her new lover before the divorce from her previous husband had been completed. (A big mistake in the 1930s.)

Another woman, Lillian Kenney, had twelve children in the ten years. (Wow!) In the end, she was disqualified because several of the children had died. She could not produce death certificates and, therefore, was unable to prove that the children were not stillborn.

However, for all their "effort" (and incredible pain) both women were awarded a consolation prize of $12,500 each.

After all court and attorney fees were subtracted, Millar's fortune had been reduced to a little over $500,000. The remaining loot was split among four women: Annie Smith, Kathleen Nagle, Lucy Timleck, and Isabel MacLean. Each had given birth to nine children during the ten-year span.

This derby was better than any horse race.

Useless? Useful? I'll leave that for you to decide.

References

The references used in writing this book are listed below. Each set of references is broken down into the two categories of *Web Links* and *Additional Resources.* Please be aware that Web pages come and go and are rarely, if ever, updated. I would not recommend using any Web page as a primary source, especially since anyone can be an expert on the Internet. The *Additional Resources,* on the other hand, are typically more reliable. These include books, magazine or newspaper articles, television shows, and any other medium not mentioned.

Unlike most written works, the references are not listed in order by author or date. Instead, I have chosen to list them in their general order of importance. References at the top of each section are, based on my experience, the best places to start your research. Those at the bottom offer less information.

Lastly, it should be fairly obvious that I have chosen to use the *SSS* method of citation. That stands for the *Steve Silverman Style* of listing sources. I have avoided the MLA or similar citation style so that I could personalize each source. I'm sure that this decision will make some English teachers out there very angry, but, hey, it's my book! After researching all of these stories over the past six years, I have been sorely disappointed by the citations listed in many other works. Their formal styles of citation tend to give every reference used equal importance, when we all know that this is never true. I cannot begin to tell you how many times I have spent hours hunting down a particular source only to be sorely disappointed in what it had to offer. I am hoping that my plain English *SSS* method of citing works will be of great help to those who wish to do further research on these topics.

PART 1: YOU'VE GOT TO BE KIDDING!

<u>MIKE, THE HEADLESS CHICKEN</u>
Web Links:
You can find out a little more about Mike at http://www.miketheheadlesschicken.org/, which is basically a promotional tool for the annual Fruita celebration. The site does have some basic information and some related materials.

"Mike the Headless Chicken more popular than Clinton" (http://ww1.salonmagazine.com/people/col/reit/1999/05/12/sn/index.html) can be found in the May 12, 1999, issue of the online magazine *Salon*.

Additional Resources:
The most complete reference on Mike can be found in *The Official Mike the Headless Chicken Book* by Teri Thomas (2000, Fruita, Colo.: Fruita Times). Written in cooperation with the Olsen's grandson Troy Waters, this book is filled with photographs, stories, letters, and everything else that one would want to know about Miracle Mike. At nearly a hundred pages, this book is an excellent source and is well worth reading. Copies can be purchased on the book's Web site at http://www.miketheheadlesschickenbook.com/ or by calling the Fruita Times at 970-858-3924. They also sell a great T-shirt with Mike pictured on it. (I bought one and love it!)

Four excellent photographs of Mike are featured in the October 22, 1945, issue of *Life* magazine. The article is titled "Headless Rooster—Beheaded chicken lives normally after freak decapitation by ax" and can be found on pages 53–54.

A brief overview on Mike's life can be found on page 2 of the May 13, 1999, issue of the *Edmonton Sun*. The article is titled "First Light/Something Bright to Start Your Day."

The May 11, 1999, issue of the *Denver Post* features an excellent article titled "Town celebrates headless critter of the '40s" by Nancy Lofholm. The follow-up article, "Fruita Remembers Mike" can be found in the May 17 issue. These articles were originally obtained from the paper's Web site, but are no longer available.

FARTMAN

Web Links:

"Le Pétomane: The Strange Life of a Fartiste" by Garrick H. S. Brown is a very detailed story on the man's talent (http:// www.retroactive.com/jan98/petomane.html).

Additional Resources:

A detailed story on Pujol can be found in the very unusual book *RE/Search Guide to Bodily Fluids* by Paul Spinrad (1994, San Francisco, Calif.: RE/Search Publications, pages 32–34.

Where did I first get this strange true story? (I couldn't make something like this up.) It's a story called "The King of Farts" from *The Best of Uncle John's Bathroom Reader* (an appropriate book for this topic) by the Bathroom Readers' Institute (1995, Berkeley, Calif.: Bathroom Readers' Institute, pages 147–50).

THE COLLYER BROTHERS

Web Links:

The *New York Daily News* offers an excellent story on the Collyer Brothers. Check out "Ghost Story: The Collyer Brothers, 1947," by Jay Maeder at http://www.nydailynews.com/manual/news/bigtown/ chap106.htm.

Additional Resources:

There is no shortage of stories on the Collyer Brothers. The hunt for Langley was quite the media sensation in its day.

A very nice summary of all of the events can be found in the April 7, 1947, issue of *Time* magazine (pages 27–28).

"Homer Collyer Dies Amid Junk, Brother Langley Can't Be Found" is an excellent story with many excerpts from an earlier interview with Langley. This story is in the Saturday, March 22, 1947, issue of the *New York Herald Tribune* (page 1, columns 2 and 3).

The following articles can all be found in the *New York Times:*

- "Homer Collyer, Harlem Recluse, Found Dead at 70" (March 22, 1947, page 1, column 5).
- "Hunt for Collyer Set for Tomorrow" (March 23, 1947, page 1, column 6).
- "Thousands Gape at Collyer House" (March 24, 1947, page 44, column 1).

- "Police Fail to Find Collyer in House" (March 25, 1947, page 27, column 1).
- "Collyer Mansion Yields Junk, Cats" (March 26, 1947, page 27, column 5).
- "Langley Collyer Is Dead, Police Say" (March 27, 1947, page 56, column 2).
- "Court Fails to Act on Collyer Estate" (March 28, 1947, page 15, column 4).
- "Resort Is Searched for Langley Collyer" (March 30, 1947, page 11, column 1).
- "3d Search Starts at Collyer House" (April 1, 1947, page 30, column 6).
- "53 Attend Burial of Homer Collyer" (April 2, 1947, page 38, column 4).
- "More Secrets Taken from Collyer Home" (April 4, 1947, page 25, column 3).
- "Collyer House Hunt to Last for Week" (April 8, 1947, page 17, column 8).
- "Body of Collyer Is Found Near Where Brother Died" (April 9, 1947, page 1, column 2).
- "Langley Collyer Dead Near Month" (April 10, 1947, page 52, column 1).
- "Langley Collyer Buried" (April 12, 1947, page 15, column 6).
- "4 Pianos Auctioned in Collyer Parlor" (June 21, 1947, page 19, column 6).
- "Collyer House to Go" (July 1, 1947, page 13, column 5).

MICHAEL MALLOY

Web Links:

The Internet is not a good source for information on Michael Malloy. The few stories that are out there are very brief and lack specific details.

If you want to save time, a condensed version of this story can be found on the page "The Story of Michael Malloy" at http://www.twisted-helices.com/music/primus/misc/malloy.html. The author of this page has based it on an older version of the story that is contained in this book and, as a result, may not be completely accurate.

Additional Resources:

An excellent summary can be found in the book *The People's Almanac #2* by David Wallechinsky and Irving Wallace (1978, New York: William Morrow, pages 41–44).

In the book *Where Death Delights* (1967, New York: American Book-Stratford Press, pages 125–38), Marshall Houts has included an entire chapter on the death of Malloy. While his account of the murder is very detailed, it has numerous inconsistencies with all of the other sources mentioned here. The name Malloy is misspelled as Molloy, some of the nicknames for Murder Trust members are interchanged, and several story details do not agree with those told by court reporters at the time. It's an excellent story to read, but one should be questioning the details while reading it.

The following articles are from the *New York Times:*

- "Insurance Murder Charged to Five" (May 13, 1933, page 28, column 2).
- "Murder Plot Seen in Another Death" (May 14, 1933, page 27, column 3).
- "Substitute Victim in Murder Found" (May 26, 1933, page 7, column 1).
- "Murder Testimony Ends" (October 18, 1933, page 44, column 3).
- "Four Men to Die for Bronx Killing" (October 20, 1933, page 38, column 2).
- "3 Die at Sing Sing for Bronx Murder" (June 8, 1934, page 44, column 4).
- "New Murphy Evidence Heard" (June 20, 1934, page 5, column 7).
- "Murphy Goes to the Chair" (July 6, 1934, page 10, column 2).

These articles are from the *New York Herald Tribune:*

- "Insurance Plot Inquiry Told of 2 More Victims" (May 13, 1933, page 26, column 4).
- "5 Are Indicted as Murderers for Insurance" (May 17, 1933, page 36, column 4).
- "Witness Called Insurance Plot Substitute Held" (May 26, 1933, page 3, column 5).
- "Hired as Killer for $150, Taxi Driver Admits" (October 11, 1933, page 3, column 2).
- "Jury Told Gas Extinguished Durable Malloy" (October 12, 1933, page 3, column 6).

- "Bastone Called Stage Manager in Malloy Death" (October 14, 1933, page 3, column 6).
- "Plotter Relates Gas Tube Exit of Durable Malloy" (October 18, 1933, page 3, column 1—next to the equally important article showing Albert Einstein arriving in the United States!).
- "Gas Verdict Stuns 4 Who Gassed Malloy" (October 20, 1933, page 3, column 1).
- "Malloy Slayers Doomed to Die Week of Nov. 20" (October 21, 1933, page 3, column 4).

THE ROOSTER BOOSTER

Web Links:

The first site that you should check out is "The Straight Dope" column on this topic written by the one and only Cecil Adams. It is not the most authoritative work on the subject, but it appears to be quite accurate (http://www.straightdope.com/classics/a5_170b.html).

"Duck! Incoming!" by Tech Sergeant Pat McKenna discusses the Air Force's firing of both fake and live chickens to test aircraft components. A discussion of methods used to scare birds away during real-life flights is also presented. Well written and very informative (http://www.af.mil/news/airman/0296/duck.htm).

A November 14, 1985, article from the *Chicago Tribune* is titled "Feathered Friends: Man Pits His Wits Against Birds That Bash into Planes." This short summary, written by Edward Humes, discusses the use of the chicken cannon at Arnold Air Force Base in Tennessee (http://home.xnet.com/~warinner/chickref.html).

Check out an excellent discussion on the accuracy of the frozen chicken story at "Thaw Before Use!" This site includes several links to "thaw before use" stories (http://www.xnet.com/~warinner/chickens.html).

Additional Resources:

Try to get your hands on the December 9, 1997, episode of *Public Eye*, which was hosted by Bryant Gumbel. This show was broadcast by CBS and showed actual footage of the Rooster Booster in action.

BALLOONING
  Web Links:
  An excellent discussion on Larry's flight can be found in the story "Up, Up, and Away!" on the Urban Legends Web site (http://www.snopes2.com/spoons/noose/balloon.htm).
  Additional Resources:
  George Plimpton has written the excellent article "The Man in the Flying Lawn Chair," which is perhaps the best summary available on Larry's life and flight (*The New Yorker*, June 1, 1998, pages 62–67).
  The December 13, 1993 (page 54), issue of *People* magazine features an article on Larry's death.

PART 2: OOPS!

THE GREAT BOSTON MOLASSES TRAGEDY
  Web Links:
  One of the best sources online is titled "The Molasses Flood of January 15, 1919" and is actually a reprint of John Mason's article that originally appeared in the January 1965 issue of *Yankee Magazine*. The story is an excellent overview of the disaster and its aftereffects (http://www.mv.com/ipusers/arcade/molasses.htm).
  Another excellent source is the Mining Co.'s *Urban Legends and Folklore* section. David Emery's December 31, 1997, story titled "Molasses Clocked at 35 mph . . . in January!" (http://urbanlegends.tqn.com/library/weekly/aa123197.htm) discusses the event and provides additional links on the Net.
  Tony Sakalauskas has prepared a great story titled "The Boston Molasses Flood of 1919" (http://maxpages.com/truetales/The_Boston_Molasses_Flood).
  Additional Resources:
  The great article "In Boston, Jan. 15 Always Sticks Out" by John Larrabee is on page 6 of the January 14, 1994, issue of *USA Today*.
  An article titled "12 Killed When Tank of Molasses Explodes" can be located in the January 16, 1919, issue of the *New York Times* (page 4, column 3) and is based on preliminary reports of the disaster.
  And, lastly, you can find an excellent interview with one of the survivors in the transcripts of the January 15, 1994, National Public

Radio broadcast. The interview, titled "Memories of Boston's 1919 Great Molasses Flood," occurred on the seventy-fifth anniversary of the accident.

CITICORP TOWER
Web Links:

Be sure to check out the excellent Web site on this story titled "William LeMessurier: The Fifty-Nine Story Crisis; A Lesson in Professional Behavior" (http://onlineethics.org/moral/LeMessurier/lem.html).

Additional Resources:

The best reference on the Citibank crisis can be easily be found by watching the excellent A&E program titled *Investigative Reports—"Fatal Flaw: A Skyscraper's Nightmare."* This program, hosted by Bill Kurtis, features interviews with all of the key players in the crisis, except the New Jersey college student whose name is lost to history.

Be sure to read the excellent article "The Fifty-Nine-Story Crisis" by Joe Morgenstern, which appears on pages 45–53 of the May 29, 1995, issue of *The New Yorker* magazine.

THE LAKE PEIGNEUR DISASTER
Web Links:

George Hollier has prepared a very nice story on Lake Peigneur and the aftereffects of the disaster. "Domes on the Range" can be found at http://www.neworleans.com/lalife/17.4.-DOMESON.html.

Additional Resources:

The *Times-Picayune* (New Orleans) is an excellent source for information on the salt dome collapse:
- "Collapsed Salt Dome Swallows Lake, Land" (November 21, 1980, section 1, page 1, column 1).
- "Hole Gobbles Everything in Sight" (November 21, 1980, section 1, page 1, column 3).
- "Mine Gurgles, Belches Noise" (November 22, 1980, section 1, page 1, column 1).
- "Mine Collapse a 'Freak,' Experts Say" (November 22, 1980, section 1, page 15, column 1).
- "Description of Cave-In Difficult" (November 22, 1980, section 1, page 15, column 1).

- "Islander Grieves for Lost Gardens, Trapped Pet Dogs" (November 22, 1980, section 1, page 15, column 5).
- "Crater: Cave-In Happened Slowly, but Full Force Not Yet Felt" (November 23, 1980, section 1, page 1, column 2).
- "Barges Pop Up as Lake Refilled" (November 24, 1980, section 1, page 1, column 2).
- "Flooded Mine Is Probed for Danger of Collapse" (November 25, 1980, section 1, page 14, column 3).
- "Flooded Salt Mine Throwing Fits" (November 26, 1980, section 2, page 3, column 1).
- "Texaco Sues in Cave-In" (November 27, 1980, section 1, page 27, column 1).
- "Salt Dome Bubbles but Stands Steady" (November 29, 1980, section 1, page 20, column 1).
- "U.S. Experts Leave Dome Cave-In Site" (December 6, 1980, section 1, page 26, column 1).
- "Suit Claims Woman Was Trapped in Salt Mine" (June 20, 1981, section 1, page 23, column 1).
- "Feds Cannot Place Blame in Salt Dome Collapse" (August 19, 1981, section 1, page 21, column 1).
- "Life Changed When the Lake Went Down the Drain" (September 29, 1981, section 2, page 8, column 1).
- "Piercing of Salt Dome to Cost Texaco, Company Millions" (July 7, 1983, section 1, page 18, column 3).
- "Life Returns to Normal on the Edge of the Abyss" (November 15, 1981, section 1, page 37, column 1).
- "Gardens Swallowed by Lake to Blossom Anew" (August 21, 1983, section 1, page 22, column 1).

The *Chicago Tribune* featured these stories:

- "Salt Mine Cave-ins Peril Area" (November 22, 1980, section 1, page 6, column 1).
- "Barges Pop Back Up as Lake Refills" (November 23, 1980, section 1, page 16, column 1).
- "Lake Survives 'Vanishing Act'" (December 14, 1980, section 3, page 21, column 3).
- "Freak Accident" (Editorial, December 16, 1980, section 5, page 2, column 1).

"Who Pulled the Plug on Lake Peigneur?" by Michael Gold is an excellent summary of the events that took place (*Science* 81, November 1981, pages 56–63).

THE RAINMAN
Web Links:
The San Diego Historical Society has a biography on Charles Hatfield at http://edweb.sdsu.edu/sdhs/bio/hatfield/hatfield.htm. An excellent photograph of Hatfield mixing up his brew accompanies the story.

The Discovery Channel's excellent Wayback Machine featured the story "What a Day! Not a Cloud in the Sky" on September 15, 1997. Go to http://www.discovery.com/area/wayback/wayback970915/wayback.html for the story and several excellent photographs.

The music magazine *An Honest Tune* dedicates a good portion of its Web site to the story about Hatfield. The index to their Hatfield material can be found at http://www.anhonesttune.com/hatfield/hatfield_idx.htm and helps to explain the meaning of the song "Hatfield" performed by the band Widespread Panic.

If you would like to read more about Hatfield's Alaskan rainmaking, be sure to check out the About.com article "The Klondike Rainmaker" at http://arcticculture.about.com/culture/arcticculture/library/yafeatures/bl-rainmaker.htm.

Additional Resources:
Clark C. Spence does an excellent job of summarizing Hatfield's career in a book appropriately titled *The Rainmakers* (1980, Lincoln, Neb.: University of Nebraska Press, pages 79–99). There is an excellent list of sources in the back of the book for additional research.

Be sure to check out the story "The Rainmaker," which appears on pages 644–47 of *The People's Almanac #3* by David Wallachinsky and Irving Wallace (1981, New York: William Morrow).

The book *Investigating the Unexplained* by Ivan T. Sanderson (1972, Englewood Cliffs, N.J.: Prentice-Hall, pages 211–28) contains an entire chapter on rainmaking and cloud-busting. Included in this chapter is an excellent article on Hatfield reprinted from the *National Enquirer.*

The March, 1998 issue of A&E's *Biography* magazine (volume 2, issue 3, page 112) contains the article "The Rain King" by David Lindsay.

The *New York Times* contains the following stories:

- "Farmers Offer Rain-Maker $3,000 an Inch for a Shower" (July 27, 1927, page 1, column 2).
- "Rainmaker Dies at 82" (April 15, 1958, page 40, column 3).
- The editorial "Rain Making" (May 15, 1905, page 8, column 4).

PART 3: INVENTIVE GENIUS

KITTY LITTER

Web Links:

Check out the "Edward Lowe Biography" at (http://www.lowe.org/history/edbio.htm) for a brief overview of his invention. This page also includes photographs of a young Ed in his Navy uniform, his 1943 Chevy coupe, and an old-time Kitty Litter point-of-purchase display.

Additional Resources:

An excellent story on this topic is the article "Cat Litter: The Inside Scoop," which can be found in the trade journal *Pet Business* (July 1996, page 48).

The National Public Radio transcript "Inventor of Kitty Litter Had Humble Beginnings" features an interview with Ed's daughter Kathy Petersen just shortly after her father's passing.

The January 19, 1995, edition of the *Los Angeles Times* features the article "The Environmental Scoop on Kitty Litter; It's Dusty, It's Dirty, but If You Use Some Clumping Brands Correctly, It Can Be Less of a Mess. But You Still Can't Flush It" by Richard Kahlenberg (page J-24).

EINSTEIN'S REFRIGERATOR

Web Links:

Be sure to check out Gene Dannen's home page at http://www.dannen.com, which is devoted to his research on Leo Szilard. Dannen is the foremost authority on the Einstein-Szilard refrigerators and devotes a good portion of his Web site to this subject.

The Exploration Network, which is the Canadian Discovery Channel, has an excellent article written by Naela Choudhary titled "Einstein's Fridge Put on Ice." You can see this story at http://www.exn.ca/Stories/1997/03/20/02.cfm.

Andrew Delano's Ph.D. thesis, "Design Analysis of the Einstein

Refrigeration Cycle," can be found on the Georgia Institute of Technology's Web site at http://www.me.gatech.edu/energy/andy/index.html.

The transcript of the series *Engines of Our Ingenuity* has a nice summary of Einstein's inventive genius. Titled "Einstein: Inventor," this short summary can be found at http://www.uh.edu/engines/epi524.htm.

Additional Resources:

The best article available on this subject is "The Einstein-Szilard Refrigerators" by Gene Dannen, which appeared in the January 1997 issue of *Scientific American* (pages 90–95). This excellent article includes many rare photographs of the refrigerator and its cooling devices.

The Winter 1991 issue of *American Heritage of Invention and Technology* magazine contains the article "Einstein the Inventor" by Thomas P. Hughes (pages 34–39). In addition to his contributions to refrigeration, this article also discusses Einstein's work in the Swiss Patent Office and his contributions to gyrocompass improvements.

THE FOOT THINGY

Web Links:

Make sure that you check out *The Genuine Brannock Device* Web site at http://www.brannock.com. Here you will find descriptions of all available Brannock Devices, a great article on the company's history, and the ability to ask an expert any questions that you may have.

Additional Resources:

The history of the Brannock Device can be found in the article "It's the whatchamacallit they use at the shoestore" by William Kates, which appeared in the May 25, 1998, issue of the *Albany Times Union*. This particular article is credited to the Associated Press, so it probably can be located in other newspapers published around the same time.

The book *Inconspicuous Consumption* by Paul Lukas (1997, New York: Random House, pages 16–17) features a two-page summary of the Brannock Device. This book is fun to read and features many objects that you probably have never thought about. Most of this particular story is reproduced on *The Daily Ardmoreite* (http://www.ardmoreite.com/stories/021797/fun/fun06a.html) Web site.

The Brannock Device has made it into the Smithsonian as part of their Modern Inventors Documentation program. You can read all about this in Berry Craig's story "Syracuse Creation Lands at Smithsonian." It appears on page 3 of the *Business Journal* published by the Central New York Business Review on August 20, 1999. He also has a story titled "Shoe-Biz Fixture Becomes a Marketing Medium," which appears on page 2 of the April 30, 1999, issue of the same journal.

Apparently Berry Craig has been making a living writing about the Brannock Device. He also wrote the excellent story "The Brannock Device: The Quintessential Example of Inconspicuous Consumption," which appears in the *Business Journal Serving Southern Tier, CNY, Mohawk Valley, Finger Lakes, North* (say that three times fast). The article is on page 10 of the May 12, 1997, issue.

AMERICA'S FIRST SUBWAY

Web Links:

Check out "Alfred Ely Beach: Beach's Bizarre Broadway Subway" at http://www.klaatu.org/klaatu11.html for a well-written story on this subject.

Another nice summary titled "Beach Pneumatic Transit" can be found at http://www.nycsubway.org/faq/earlysubway.html.

Additional Resources:

The best source out there on the pneumatic subway is *Labyrinths of Iron: A History of the World's Subways* by Benson Bobrick (1981, New York: Newsweek Books, pages 169–94).

If you can locate a copy at your local library, the February 24, 1912, issue of *Scientific American* has an excellent story titled "New York's First Subway" (volume 106, pages 176–77). Many great photographs accompany this article.

The Winter 1997 issue of *American Heritage of Invention & Technology* features another excellent article titled "New York's Secret Subway," which was written by Oliver E. Allen (pages 44–48).

The *New-York Daily Tribune* has an article titled "Lull in Subway Talk," which discusses Beach's subway (February 4, 1912, page 7, column 1).

The October 1997 issue of *Scientific American* features an article titled "13 Vehicles That Went Nowhere" on page 65. To no one's surprise, Beach's pneumatic subway is one of the unlucky thirteen.

A large number of *New York Times* articles can be found on this subject. Only the best ones are listed here:

- "First Subway 40 Years Ago: Started in Lower Broadway and Trains Were to Run by Air Pressure" (February 4, 1912, page 15, column 1).

- "Broadway Tube Proposed in '49: Alfred Ely Beach, Who Devised Shield Method of Subway Building, Sponsored the Project Then" (September 12, 1926, section 3, page 12, column 1).
- "Plaque in City Hall Station to Mark First Subway Site" (September 15, 1932, page 23, column 5).
- "The First Subway" (September 17, 1932, page 14, column 3).
- "New York's First Subway," editorial (February 27, 1940, page 20, column 3).
- "First Subway Here Was Like a Popgun: Opened 80 Years Ago, It Shot Its Car, Full of Passengers, with Compressed Air" (February 25, 1950, page 19, column 1).

VASELINE

Web Links:

For a list of uses for Vaseline, check out http://www.wackyuses.com/jelly.html.

Additional Resources:

If you want to learn more about the history of Vaseline (and other related items) check out the great book *Panati's Extraordinary Origins of Everyday Things* by Charles Panati (1987, New York: Harper and Row).

Two additional excellent sources are *They All Laughed . . .* by Ira Flatow (1993, New York: HarperPerennial, pages 152–55) and *Why Didn't I Think of That?* by Allyn Freeman and Bob Golden (1997, New York: John Wiley & Sons, pages 78–82).

HEDY LAMARR

Web Links:

There is certainly no shortage of information available when dealing with a person as famous as Hedy Lamarr. The best Web resources are described below for your reference.

George Antheil's son Chris Beaumont has prepared the most complete site on the patent, which can be found at "Secret Communications System: The Fascinating Story of the Lamarr/Antheil Spread-Spectrum Patent" at http://www.ncafe.com/chris/pat2/index.html.

There is an excellent summary of Hedy Lamarr's life, career, and invention on the nicely designed Web site "Hommage à Hedy Lamarr," which can be found at http://www.hedylamarr.at/indexe.html.

Karin Hanta has written an excellent story about Lamarr's invention for the magazine *Austria Kultur*. The story "Beauty and the Brains" can be found on the Web at http://www.austriaculture.net/AustrKult161.975.html/BeautyBrain.html.

"Did You Know?" at http://www.astr.ua.edu/4000WS/didyouknow.1.html offers a short history on Lamarr's invention. The story is a brief summary of the AP article from March 1997.

The "George Antheil Biography" at http://www.schirmer.com/composers/antheil_bio.html offers a nice summary of his life and key works.

Additional Resources:

Space does not permit the listing of every source used in the preparation of this story. Below are the articles and books that were most helpful. Additional sources can easily be found by searching your local library.

Perhaps the best article on Lamarr's invention can be found in the Spring 1997 issue of *American Heritage of Invention & Technology*. This cover story is titled "Advanced Weaponry of the Stars" and is written by Hans-Joachim Braun. The story can be found on pages 10–16.

There is an excellent article titled "I Guess They Just Take and Forget about a Person," which appears in the May 14, 1990, issue of *Forbes* magazine (pages 136–38). The story focuses on Ms. Lamarr's invention and includes a short interview.

The short article "Hedy Lamarr Inventor" appeared in the October 1, 1941, issue of the *New York Times* (page 24, column 1).

The *Chicago Tribune* did a nice piece on her invention titled "Brainy Beauty" (March 31, 1997, section 5, page 1, column 2).

The October 9, 1993, issue of the *Economist* (volume 329, issue 7832, page 92) features a story titled "Spread Thin." The article describes the link between Ms. Lamarr's invention and Cincinnati Microwave's efforts to produce frequency-hopping cordless telephones.

A very interesting article titled "Would You Believe I Was a Famous Star? It's the Truth!" describes the rise and fall of Hedy Lamarr's career. A photograph of her at age 54 is included. You can find this story in the August 23, 1970, issue of the *New York Times* (section 2, page 11, column 1).

The October 1, 1937, issue of the *New York Times* (page 18, column 7) has a short story titled "Actors and Singers Here on Normandie," which describes the arrival of Hedy Kiesler in the United

States and states that her new name will be . . . you guessed it . . . Hedy Lamarr. This story actually contradicts the blurb in her autobiography of how she got the name.

Of course, this list would be incomplete without the mention of her controversial autobiography, *Ecstasy and Me* (1966, New York: Bartholemew House). The book is currently out of print but many copies abound. (I borrowed it from the public library.) The book is easy reading and holds together well for the first two thirds of its 300-plus pages (but makes no mention of her patent). This is a riches to rags tale and would better be titled "How to Blow 30 Million Bucks Without Trying." There are many mentions of sexual encounters in this book (with both men and women), but names are changed to protect those involved. While not innocent in any sense of the word, the book is fairly mild when compared to what people read today.

Lastly, be sure to check out a copy of her patent, which can be found in many public and university libraries around the world.

THE ZIPPER

Web Links:

A brief biography on Judson can be found in the Inventor of the Week Archives at http://web.mit.edu/invent/www/inventors1-Q/judson.html.

About.com offers an excellent overview of the zipper's history. Includes a scan of the original zipper patent (http://inventors.tqn.com/science/inventors/library/weekly/aa082497.htm).

Additional Resources:

The best source available is *Zipper: An Exploration in Novelty* by Robert Friedel (1994, New York: W. W. Norton). This book nicely traces the history of the zipper from its invention, through its perfection, to its modern use.

Be sure to check out pages 8–16 of the Summer 1994 issue of *American Heritage of Invention and Technology* for a detailed cover story on zippers titled "The History of the Zipper?" also written by Friedel.

<u>NIKOLA TESLA</u>
Web Links:

The Internet is filled with information on Nikola Tesla. Use your favorite search engine to find additional information on the man and his life. Here are a few of my favorites:

"Science Hobbyist" offers a Tesla page at http://www.eskimo.com/~billb/tesla/tesla.html. Here you will find an excellent listing of links to other Tesla Web pages. A great place to start.

PBS has created an excellent Web site to accompany the *Tesla—Master of Lightning* documentary (http://www.pbs.org/tesla/).

Nikola Tesla once had a town and coal mine named after him. Dan Mosier, a Tesla historian, has done an excellent job of preparing the history of Tesla, California (http://cmug.com/~minesroad/Tesla.html).

Additional Resources:

Be sure to read the excellent book *Tesla: Man Out of Time* by Margaret Cheney (1981, New York: Dell Publishing).

Barnes and Noble in New York published two books by Tesla himself. The first, *My Inventions* (1982), is a compilation of six articles written by Tesla for the magazine *Electrical Experimenter* in 1919. The second, *The Inventions, Researches, and Writings of Nikola Tesla* (1995), is a reprint of an 1893 book on Tesla's landmark work and is very technical in nature.

PART 4: HMMM

<u>GEORGE WASHINGTON</u>
Web Links:

Nick Pahys Jr. runs the Presidential Museum in Hartsgrove, Ohio, and is the foremost expert on John Hanson. The museum's Web site is located at http://www2.suite224.net/~pahysltd/.

"America's First President—John Hanson" by Harry V. Martin is perhaps the most detailed summary of Hanson's life on the Internet (http://www.sonic.net/sentinel/usa7.html).

Additional Resources:

I was able to locate three old books on the man at the University of Albany Library:

John Hanson of Mulberry Grove by J. Bruce Kremer (1938, New York: A. & C. Boni).

John Hanson and the Inseparable Union; An Authentic Biography of a Revolutionary Leader, Patriot and Statesman by Jacob A. Nelson (1939, Boston: Meador Publishing).

John Hanson, Our First President by Seymour W. Smith (1932, New York: Brewer, Warren & Putnam).

EMPEROR NORTON 1

Web Links:

The Net is loaded with stories on Emperor Norton. Here are just a few:

"Emperor Norton" (http://www.zpub.com/sf/history/nort.html) offers a brief timeline of his life plus numerous links and images.

The site "Emperor Norton's Archives" (http://www.notfrisco.com/nortoniana/) gives a great summary of his various proclamations plus links and additional Emperor Norton stories.

The site "Joshua Abraham Norton" (http://www3.pbs.org/weta/thewest/wpages/wpgs400/w4norton.htm) discusses how he was the basis for the character of the king in Mark Twain's (Samuel Clemens') classic *Huckleberry Finn*.

Additional Resources:

William Drury has written a great book on the emperor. It is titled *Norton I, Emperor of the United States* (1986, New York: Dodd, Mead). At 200-plus pages, this book is very well researched and is a pleasure to read.

The January 10, 1880, issue of the *New York Times* (page 5, column 2) contains Norton's obituary. It's hard to believe that he was so famous that he would command such a large article in a New York newspaper at that time.

Jed Stevenson's "Coins" article in the December 9, 1990, issue of the *New York Times* (section 1, page 84, column 1) features a brief overview of Norton's life plus a discussion of the value of his notes.

A large number of photographs of the emperor can be found in the book *The Forgotten Characters of Old San Francisco* by Robert Ernest Cowan, Anne Bancroft, and Addie L. Ballou (1964, Los Angeles: Ward Richie Press, originally published in 1938).

The February 1936 issue of *Reader's Digest* (volume 28, pages 23–27) features a biography on Emperor Norton. Note: Some of this article's information seems to differ from all the other sources used in the preparation of this story.

An excellent article titled "The Strange Story of Emperor Norton" by David Warren Ryder appears in the August 11, 1945, issue of the *Saturday Evening Post* (volume 218, page 35).

Another excellent article, "Emperor Norton I," by Joan Parker, appears in the December 1976 issue of *American Heritage* magazine (pages 84–85).

PENNIES FOR COLLEGE

Web Links:

The Urban Legends Archive features a story titled "Cent to College" (http://snopes.com/college/records/cent.htm). This page presents much of the same information described in this story.

Additional Resources:

The original Bob Greene article "Mr. Hayes, Your Penny Is in the Mail" appeared in the September 6, 1987, issue of the *Chicago Tribune* (section 5, page 1, column 1).

Bob Greene's follow-up story, "Ask and Ye Shall Receive, Indeed" can be found in the October 4, 1987, issue of the *Chicago Tribune* (section 5, page 1, column 1).

The October 26, 1987, issue of *Jet* magazine contains the article "Plea for Pennies Turns Up $14,000 for College Student Attending U. Of Illinois" (volume 73, number 5, page 24).

FU-GO

Web Links:

"Balloon Bomber" describes how a man named Yoshiji Ohsawa helped build the balloons while still a teenager in school. A description of the balloon bombing campaign can also be found here. "Balloon Bomber" is located at http://www.af.mil/news/airman/0298/bomb.htm.

The History House Web site has a two-part story on the Fu-Go project. The first part is titled "The Jet Stream Gets Drafted" and the second is "Balloons II: The Winds of Fortune" (http://www.historyhouse.com).

Additional Resources:

Without a doubt, the best source available on the Fu-Go project is the book *Japan's World War II Balloon Bomb Attacks on North America* by Robert C. Mikesh (1973, Washington, D.C: Smithsonian Institution Press). This work is well researched and features a large number of photographs of the balloons, the Japanese launch sites, and the American recoveries.

The journal *North Dakota History* (vol. 64, no. 1, Winter 1997, pages 21–26) contains an excellent article titled "The Japanese Balloon Bomb Campaign in North Dakota." This article has some excellent photographs and a detailed map of all the United States sightings. The journal can be ordered from the State Historical Society of North Dakota.

"The Year They Firebombed the West" by John McDowell is an excellent source on this subject. It appears in the May/June 1993 issue of *American Forests* (pages 22–23).

Another well-researched article titled "The Fu-Go Project" by Carmine A. Prioli was featured in the April/May issue of *American Heritage* magazine (volume 33, number 3, pages 88–92).

The History Channel occasionally broadcasts two different shows on the Fu-Go campaign. The first—"Secrets of WWII—Japan's Last Secret Weapon"—is the better of the two. The second—"In Search of History—U.S. Invaded"—devotes only one segment to the Fu-Go program.

BAT BOMBS

Web Links:

Good luck trying to find information on this unusual project on the Internet. Bits and pieces of the story can be found, but little is worth looking at. There is a Dave Barry story from 1990 titled "It's a Bird . . . It's a Plane . . . It's—Trout" floating around the Net, but it is difficult to locate. This story contains a reprint of a story titled "The Bat Bombers" by C. V. Glines, which had originally appeared in the October 1990 issue of *Air Force* magazine.

Additional Resources:

The most complete work on this topic is the book *Bat Bomb: World War II's Other Secret Weapon* by Jack Couffer (1992, Austin: University of Texas Press). When I say complete, I mean complete. At nearly 250 pages, this book chronicles the whole project from start to finish as seen through the eyes of the author, who just happened to be one of the members of the team that developed the bombs.

I first read about this story in an article titled "Bat's Away!" by Joe Michael Feist, which appeared in the April/May 1982 issue of *American Heritage* magazine (volume 33, number 3, pages 92-94).

Although short on content, the article "Incendiary Bats" from the February 16, 1948, issue of *Life* magazine (volume 24, number 7, pages 45–48) features five excellent photographs from the project.

PART 5: INCREDIBLE STORIES OF SURVIVAL

THE *TITANIC*
Web Links:
The transcript of the NOVA episode "*Titanic*'s Lost Sister" (http://www.pbs.org/wgbh/nova/transcripts/2402titanic.html) describes the search for the *Britannic*. An interview with a survivor of the lifeboat tragedy is documented, along with a description of Violet Jessop's ordeal.

Use your favorite search engine to find out general information on the *Titanic* (there is no shortage of Web sites), *Olympic,* and *Britannic*.
Additional Resources:
If you would like more information on this story, then the best source is from Violet herself. Check out the book *Titanic Survivor: The Newly Discovered Memoirs of Violet Jessop Who Survived both the* Titanic *and* Britannic *Disasters* by Violet Jessop and edited by John Maxtone-Graham (1997, Dobbs Ferry, N.Y.: Sheridan House). This manuscript was written in 1934 and documents both disasters. Note that this is an autobiography, so only a third of the book is devoted to the disasters. If you are looking for details from an actual survivor, this is the place to look.

POON LIM
Web Links:
Sorry, but no detailed information about Poon Lim could be located on the Web.
Additional Resources:
Ruthanne Lum McCunn has written an entire book on Poon Lim's ordeal titled *Sole Survivor* (1985, various publishers). The author considers this book to be a fictional re-creation, although the actual events have not been changed.

The great article "Chinese Will Get High British Honor" can be found on page 6 of the Saturday, July 17, 1943, issue of the *New York Times*.

A second *New York Times* article "132-Day Drift Described" can be found in the Tuesday, May 25, 1943, issue on page 12.

The initial report of his rescue, announced by the British Parliament, can be found in a three-paragraph article titled "Alone on a Raft for 130 Days" on page 4 of the Monday, April 19, 1943, issue of *The Times* (London).

MOUNT PELÉE

Web Links:

Several nice photographs of the eruption can be seen at http://volcano.und.nodak.edu/vwdocs/volc_images/img_mt_pelee.html.

The United States Geological Survey has put together the short summary "1902 Eruption of Mont Pelée, West Indies" at http://vulcan.wr.usgs.gov/Volcanoes/WestIndies/Pelee/description_1902_eruption.html.

Additional Resources:

The most complete summary of the eruption can be found in the book *The Day the World Ended* by Gordon Thomas and Max Morgan Witts (1969, New York: Stein and Day). At nearly 300 pages, this work thoroughly examines all of the events that took place leading up to the deadly eruption.

I first came across this story in the book *Volcanoes* by Peter Francis (1976, New York: Penguin Books, pages 81–93).

Volcanoes of the Earth by Fred M. Bullard (1984, Austin: University of Texas Press, pages 119–34) offers an excellent historical review of eruption.

A. L. Koster, the first man to photograph the disaster, describes his experience in the article "City of the Dead," which appeared in the October 1956 issue of *Natural History* magazine (pages 412–15). This article includes ten photographs, including one of Ciparis, although the author is one of the few to claim that the prisoner never had a death sentence.

The August 1961 issue of *American Heritage* magazine contains the excellent story "Prelude to Doomsday" by Lately Thomas. It includes the same picture of Ciparis as the *Natural History* article above, except that the caption gives his name as Ludger Sylbaris. (He is referred to as Raoul Sarteret in a few other other works.)

Earthquakes and Volcanoes by John Gribbin (1978, New York: Bison Books) contains lots of great photos of the volcano's aftermath.

For some fascinating reports on the story, check out the many articles that appeared in the *New York Times* starting on May 9, 1902, and running for several weeks after.

PART 6: UNBELIEVABLE!

GADSBY

Web Links:

A good summary of Wright's efforts and other similar works can be found on the page titled "Reduced English" (http://www.lhup.edu/~dsimanek/eprime.htm).

Additional Resources:

Basically, the only place to start researching this topic is by getting your hands on the actual book _Gadsby: A Story of Over 50,000 Words Without Using the Letter "E"_ by Ernest Vincent Wright (1939, Los Angeles: Wetzel Publishing). This is a tough book to find and is highly valued among book collectors. I was able to locate a copy in an out-of-state library through an interlibrary loan. I was put on a waiting list for several months before actually receiving it.

A short summary can be found in the book _The People's Almanac #2_ by David Wallechinsky and Irving Wallace (1978, New York: William Morrow, page 1230).

A three-paragraph story on this book can be found in the article titled "Letter 'E' Is Not Used in 50,110 Word Novel" which appeared in the March 24, 1937, issue of the _New York Times_ (page 27, column 3).

A nice description of Wright's novel can be found on page 219 of the book _Reader's Digest Facts and Fallacies_ (1988, Pleasantville, N.Y.: The Reader's Digest Association).

NIAGARA FALLS—PART 1, PART 2

Web Links:

Can't visit the falls? Then check out the live pictures on the "Niagara FallsCam Picture Page" at http://www.fallsview.com/English/pages/fallscam.shtml.

Be sure to check out December 3, 1997, Cool Fact of the Day at http://features.learningkingdom.com/fact/archive/1997/12/03.html for more on this story.

Additional Resources:

Where did I get this story? Check out the book _Geology of our Romantic Niagara_ by A. H. Tiplin (1988, Niagara Falls, Canada: The Niagara Falls Heritage Foundation, pages 149–50).

Another source is the book *Niagara: A History of the Falls* by Pierre Berton. Starting on page 56, there is a great summary of the bridge/kite story, which includes a discussion of the falls running dry (1992, New York: Kodansha America).

A brief summary of this can be found in the book *Water Over the Falls: 101 of the Most Memorable Events at Niagara Falls* by Paul Gromosiak (1996, Western New York Wares). Oddly, this strange event is considered to be the fiftieth most memorable event and can be found on pages 41–42. Personally, I would think that it should be number one. But then, I didn't write the book.

A special thanks to the librarians at the Buffalo Public Library who helped me locate two great articles on this subject. The first is titled "Remarkable Phenomenon" and appears in the March 31, 1848, issue of the *Buffalo Morning Express* (volume 3, number 683, page 2, column 3). The second is "Wonderful Fall of Water," which can be found in the April 5, 1848, issue of the *Buffalo Daily Courier* (volume 14, number 81, page 3, column 1).

THE *AL-KUWAIT*

Web Links:

A brief summary of this story can be found on the *Timelab 2000* Web site (http://www.smash.com/seg/timelab/stories/099donald.html). Perhaps you have seen the accompanying television segment: "Donald Duck Saves the Day" on the History Channel? The segment is only about one minute long, but does feature actual footage from the event.

Additional Resources:

The best summary of this event can be found in the book *The 20th Century* by David Wallechinsky (1995, New York: Little, Brown, page 585).

Check out the article "Transport News: Plan by Harlee" in the *New York Times* (March 8, 1965, page 58, column 1). Several paragraphs on this topic can be found here, although Donald Duck is never mentioned.

A brief article titled "Plastic Bubbles Help Refloat Capsized Ship" appears in the April 1965 issue of *Popular Science* magazine (pages 118–19). Two frames of the actual Donald Duck comic and four photographs of the actual salvage operation are presented.

THE BABY DERBY

Web Links:

An excellent detailed summary of the whole derby can be found on the Urban Legends Reference Pages at http://www.snopes.com/ pregnant/babyrace.htm.

Additional Resources:

The most complete reference available on this topic is the book *The Great Stork Derby* by Mark M. Orkin (1981, Don Mills, Ont.: General Publishing). This 300-plus page book is filled with information on Millar, the contestants, and the endless court cases.

Check *out Panati's Extraordinary Endings of Practically Everything and Everybody* by Charles Panati (1989, New York: Harper and Row). This story is included in both the text version and on the audiocassette.

The October 20, 1934, issue of *Newsweek* features an excellent article titled "Baby Race: Toronto Mothers Compete for $500,000 Prize," which details this strange competition. Three photographs are included. The article can be found on page 21.

A second *Newsweek* article, "Canada: $500,000 Practical Joke Breeds a Baby Marathon," appeared in the October 31, 1936, issue on pages 16–17. Several paragraphs from Millar's will are quoted here. In addition, the lives of each of the winners is described in detail.

Over twenty articles were printed in the *New York Times* during the final years of this competition. Only the most significant are listed below:

The September 8, 1935, article "$500,000 Carried by Toronto Stork" appears in section 2 (page 1, column 2). This provides a nice summary of Millar's will and the baby race.

On February 13, 1938 (section 2, page 2, column 2), an article titled "Four Mothers of Nine Win Shares in $500,000 Stork Derby Cash" details the winners of the race. The article also describes the two other women who were disqualified.

"Stork Derby Prize Awarded 4 Women" appeared in the March 20, 1938, *New York Times* on page 20, column 3. This article presents the final outcome of the contest after all the legal challenges were resolved.